Women Up

Women United in Praise
Stories of Healing, Deliverance and Restoration

Vanessa Moore-Bulnes

*w*ith Family and Friends

Women UP- Women United in Praise
Stories of Healing, Deliverance and Restoration

Copyright © 2014 by Vanessa Moore-Bulnes
ISBN-13:978-0615999807 ((TAP) Tender Arms Productions)
ISBN-10:0615999808

All rights reserved. No part of this book may be reproduced or transmitted in any form or by any means, electronic or mechanical, including photocopying, recording, or by any information storage and retrieval, system without permission in writing from the copyright owner.

All scripture quotations are taken from the King James Version of the Bible. All rights reserved.

Cover artwork: Creative by Design
Photographer: Eric Marshall (back cover)
Poem: Crack Addition - Author Unknown
Poem: Hell? Ruth Jackson-Copyright © 2014

Women Up

Women United in Praise
Stories of Healing, Deliverance and Restoration

This book is dedicated to my Pastor and my Bishop - J.W. Macklin and my phenomenal First Lady - Missionary Vanessa J. Macklin (Glad Tidings COGIC). Thank you both for allowing me to serve the women of Glad Tidings in ministry through the Women's Support Group from which this book was inspired. Thank you both for being examples to the believers in word and in deed.

Thank you, to my husband Richard (*baby*), my children; Travares, Benjamin, Shekinah and my family in Greensboro, North Carolina for encouraging and supporting me.

Vanessa Moore-Bulnes

My Song of Praise
"Nobody but Jesus"
Kelly Price

Women Up
Women United in Praise
Stories of Healing, Deliverance and Restoration
Is a collection of inspirational stories
about amazing women from the
east coast to the west coast.
Women who have been healed from cancer
and delivered from various forms of abuse
(domestic, substance, sexual).
Women who have had relationships restored.
Women who have survived divorce
and the death of loved ones.
Women who believe their life stories will
help and encourage others.
(Revelation 12:11)

****

Women Up
Women United in Praise
"To God for the things He has done"

Each story comes with a personal introduction from the author and editor. Each story is supported by its own set of scripture references, pages for journaling your personal reflections and an inspirational *song of praise* title at each end. Use this book as a devotional guide or as an evangelistic tool to introduce someone else to the God who can heal, deliver and restore.

Vanessa Moore-Bulnes

*w*ith Family and Friends

Contents

Introduction

Prologue

Poem: *Crack Addiction*

Chapter One
Marie..*1*

Chapter Two
Gloria..*6*

Chapter Three
Betty..*15*

Chapter Four
Margo..*26*

Chapter Five
Juanita...*36*

Chapter Six
Shelley...*51*

Chapter Seven
Loretta...*62*

Chapter Eight
Ashli..*70*

Chapter Nine
Meredith..*78*

Chapter Ten
Holly..*86*

Poem: *Hell?*

Epilogue

Introduction

In October of 1999 the Lord Jesus Christ blessed me to coordinate a women's conference with the central theme being unity. At the time it seemed like an overwhelming task but the God who impregnated me with the vision also assured me that he would be with me to carry it full term.

The conference began on a Friday night and concluded that Sunday morning. The conference theme was Women of Unity and Praise or Women UP "Fulfilling our Purpose and Destiny." Our scripture text was Acts 2:1..."*and they were all with one accord in one place.*" In the following verses 2-4 it speaks of how "*suddenly there came a sound from heaven as of a rushing mighty wind, and it filled the house where they were sitting* (praising, dancing) *and they were all filled with the Holy Ghost.*"

Imagine...the word of God coming to life during a church service filled with women united in praise to God for helping us move into discovering and fulfilling our purpose and destiny in Him. Something can be said about the move of God's presence when we are all on one accord. When I was praying about a title for this book that conference theme from 15 years ago was brought to my remembrance.

As I embarked on the awesome task of exercising my gift as a writer the same God that supported me through the conference reminded me that He would be with through this project as well. "Jesus Christ the same yesterday, today and forever" (Hebrews 13:8).

In 2007 as I sat on the pews of my new church home Glad Tidings Church of God in Christ (Hayward, California) the Lord spoke to me again and I was moved to begin a women's support group. With the blessings of my pastor and first lady that ministry began meeting once a week and we did so for five years.

Once sisters, women and friends entered the doors of our meeting location they found love, guidance, healing and deliverance in a safe and confidential setting. Many of their experiences were common not only in our meetings but throughout the sanctuary and our community as well.

And...and...regardless of whether they lived on the east coast like my niece Benita, my sister Marie, my friends Gloria and Betty...God in His awesomeness is not restricted by geography because He worked in their lives the same way He did in the lives of my friends three thousand miles away...here on the west coast.

Hence **Women UP-Women United in Praise-** *Stories of Healing, Deliverance and Restoration* was conceived. Over the past twenty - eight years as a born again believer I have sat on the pews of innumerable Sunday morning services and Tuesday night bible studies and noonday prayer meetings and Friday night Holy Ghost services.

Not only that but I have served in almost every church ministry from children's church to the usher board, to singing in the choir, as well as from women's, singles and marriage ministries. Down through those years I have been inspired by my personal interactions with my sisters in Christ, my sister friends and girlfriends and my BFFs. Women whose lives reveal a fortitude that can only come from the true and living God. These stories and testimonies of how they have been healed, delivered and restored is an awesome testament to the power of our God... to those who know Him and those of you who do not.

As you turn through the pages of this book you will become acquainted with women who have stood regal and strong even in the midst of adversity. I admired the strength and fortitude that I saw in these women who continued in their relationships and marriages to men who were abusive or unfaithful until God made that way of escape. Women who were challenged to love their children and care for their homes while battling illnesses or addictions.

Addictions that stripped them of their identities as confirmed in the *Crack Addiction Poem* but were healed, delivered and restored as witnessed in the poem *Hell?* Women who yet continued to adorn themselves in their choir robes and usher uniforms as they stood on their post while all hell was breaking out at home, on their jobs and yes even in their ministries. As a prologue to this book I included a letter of true confessions from a dear family member who was woman enough to admit God is still working on her.

To all of these **Women UP**...I say thank you for giving me the opportunity to share your life in book form. Thank you for entrusting me with your inner most delicacies, knowing that God would be glorified and that the body of Christ would be edified and unbelievers would be hungry and thirsty for more of our God. Thank you for pushing me into fulfilling my purpose and my destiny as an author.

Key Words

- Healing – the process of making or becoming sound or healthy again.

- Deliverance – the state of being saved from something dangerous or unpleasant.

- Restoration – the act or process of returning something to its original condition by repairing it, cleaning it, etc. :The act of bringing back something that existed before.

- Purpose – the reason for which something is done or created or for which something exists.

- Destiny – what happens in the future: the things that someone or something will experience in the future. :A power that is believed to control what happens in the future.

(Merriam-Webster Dictionary-on-line)

Hi Auntie,

   Congratulations! Congratulations! To God be the Glory! I'm truly overwhelmed with the endeavors you've accomplished, amplified by your consistency on so many levels for so many years. I'm writing this letter because what you stand for has not only intensified my mindset positively, but it has changed the way I react to actions.
   I spoke highly of Aunt Marie and Aunt Ola too late, as well as Grandma Algie Vee at their home goings. I won't make those mistakes again. Looking back over my life, I never knew how blessed I was in my mess. I remember questioning God to you so many times, never believing it was his grace and mercy that let me voice those negative thoughts.
   Today the thoughts pertain to how I can tell others how good how great how undeniable his love is. The anxiety of wanting to be beautiful inside consumes me, right along with asking and praying that God has forgiven me for the lies, the terrible things I've done in my past.
   I realize that I can only praise Him and tell others of my experiences. Instead of going to friends or family with my struggles, I've continued to go to church.
   New Hope has been such an instrumental part of me finding purpose. Pastor Allison and Mrs. Allison have brought me out of my spiritual shyness. I am no longer afraid to share my love for God in front of others. Mrs. Allison is truly a blessing in my life. I feel the sincerity in her spirit something that was needed in order for me to release and rejoice completely.
   I wanted to express the delay in my testimony. Being real and totally honest about my past is something I really

have to take methodically. When you asked me to do a short story I was truly honored. It was called from "Chaos to Calm". The more my words hit the paper the more I relived those years. My flesh wasn't ready. The memories touched on sexual content, theft, hatred and just stuff I mentally wasn't prepared to reveal to others, let alone myself.

    Lastly, I'm still fighting the battle of life, although it's not mine to fight. God reveals some things profound as well as common sensibility. I'm blessed to be alert and aware that He's the master of it all. I continue to stand still until His will is clear. At this time in my life I don't feel I'm where I should be in order to contribute an overcoming testimony. God is still working on me.

Sincerely Benita

"I love you Nita"

Crack Addition Poem

I destroy homes...I tear families apart. I take
your children ...and that's just the start.
I'm more costly than diamonds, more precious than gold.
The sorrow I bring is a sight to behold.

If you need me remember, I'm easily found...
I live all around you... in schools and in town.
I live with the rich... I live with the poor...
I live down the street...maybe even next door.

I am made in such ways... you can shoot me or smoke...
I used to be called "cocaine...or coke"
The sound that I make, when you're inhaling my stench...
is how my name "Crack" came to be...(perfect sense)

My power is awesome; try me, you'll see...But if you do,
you may never break free. Just try me once, and I may
let you go...But try me twice, and I'll own your soul.
When "I" possess you, you'll steal and you'll lie.
You'll do what you have to, just to get "high".

The crimes you commit, for my narcotic charms...
Will be worth the pleasure you'll feel in your lungs,
nose and arms. You'll lie to your mother, you'll steal
from your dad... When you see their tears...you should feel sad.

But you will forget your morals...and how you were raised...
I'll be your "conscience" ...I'll teach you "my ways."
I'll take kids from parents, and parents from kids.
I turn people from "GOD"...and separate friends.
I'll take everything from you...your looks and
your pride. I'll be with you ALWAYS...right by
your side.

You'll give up everything ...your family, your home...
your friends...your money...then you'll be all alone.
I'll take and take, till you have nothing more to give...
When I'm finished with you...you'll be lucky to live.

If you try me, be warned...this is no "game"...if given the chance...I'll drive you insane!
I'll ravish your body...I'll control your mind...I'll own you completely"... your "soul" will be mine!

The nightmares I'll give you, while lying in bed...
The voices you'll hear...from inside your head...
The sweats, the shakes... the "visions" you'll see...
I want you to know...these are ALL "gifts from me".

But then it's too late, and you'll know in your heart...
That you are MINE...and we shall not part...
You'll regret that you tried me...they always do...
But YOU came to ME...Not "I" to you...

You knew this would happen... many times you were told...
But you challenged my "power"...and chose to be "bold".
You could have said "no"...and just walked away...
If you could live that day over...now what would you say?

I'll be your "master"...and you'll be my slave...
I'll even go with you...when you go to your grave.
Now that you have met me...what will you do?
Will you try me or not? It's all up to you...
I can bring you more misery than words can tell...

Come take my hand...let me lead you to **HELL!**

Author Unknown

Chapter One
Marie

Marie She was my big sister. We all have heard the saying that a person who has passed away is still with us in spirit. This can be said about my sister Marie. She was born October 2, 1949 in Greensboro North Carolina to the late Jimmie and Algie Moore. She was the seventh of nine children...6 girls and 3 boys. She met and married Timothy Evans and to our family that was the beginning of all of her sorrows. Her husband preceded her in death and to their union two children were born Timothy Jr. and Tiffany.

There was standing room only at her home going celebration. I spoke at the service and was reflective of the impact that she had on my life. Our parents had their first seven children and nine years later our sister Cheryl and then me. She was like our link to the world outside of mama's house.

Marie hired me for my first job at the Carolina Nursing Center as a kitchen aid in the foodservice department when I was 16 years old. She was instrumental in me, Cheryl and our three nieces all similar in age...the self-proclaimed Five Bold Women getting our ears pierced the old school way with the needle and thread, *"ouch"*. She taught us how to tint our hair auburn red and she turned us on to our first joint. She taught us how to party responsibly and we all partied together.

Over the years Marie obtained numerous career related awards and certificates. She had a beautiful voice and sang in several choirs at the New Hope Missionary Baptist Church, where she was a faithful member for over 30 years. She was also a member of the Women Walking by Faith organization.

Marie was a sports fanatic who loved to play tennis and she swam like a fish. The beach was her second home. She was a kind, loving and caring person who put others before herself. Marie never met a stranger and she would open her heart and home to anyone.

She loved and celebrated life to the fullest. She was affectionately called "Cleo" by her close friends from the movie Cleopatra Jones because she was tall, bold and beautiful like the character in the movie. She loved Gladys Knight and The Pips so much so that she took ownership of the name Gladys and named herself Marie Gladys. Some called her Ms. Ross which was short for Diana Ross because she was one classy lady; regardless of what you called Marie she would answer.

Marie's untimely death has caused a void in everyone's life which will never be filled. Her death was untimely because she passed three weeks after her husband died. We thought for sure that once he was gone she would finally be free to live the kind of life her family thought she should live.

They were married thirty plus years. As soon as she said "I do" he didn't. He didn't work, he didn't go to church, he did not love honor and cherish her. For the most part he was in and out of prison. If you know anything about loving someone locked up it's practically like you are a prisoner as well.

She was a faithful wife who visited him regularly and did what she had to do to support his drug habit while he was locked up. He was the kind of man that brought a woman down instead of building her up. Every car she worked hard to get he wrecked it or traded it for drugs, every house or apartment she got he would get them kicked out.

She would follow him anywhere. It seemed like she really believed in him. Around 1988 he decided to relocate his family to Florida having no job and no shelter. They took their young babies and as he said they lived on the land. By the time they made their way back home to North Carolina they were totally emaciated.

Without any warning about her appearance when I saw her I broke down in tears. Someone asked if I was crying because I was glad to see her or was it because of the way she looked. It was heart-breaking to see my sister look like that. But like the character she was nicknamed after Cleo would always bounce back. She was a survivor and did what she had to do within the law to provide for her children and husband.

Sitting around our mother's house we still joke about her at times because she was the original meals on wheels. Marie always had a job in the food service industry. Like pulling a rabbit out of a hat she would pull a dish from under the hood of her car or a hot meal out of the trunk. She was always a favorite participant at barbeques and fish fries. That's when her true culinary skills would come forth and during those times she dominated the grill and or the electric frying pan. Although a couple of times she left us wondering at Thanksgiving dinner what that mysterious looking dish...the one we dared not touch was.

We know that she took her vows seriously that's the only way we could determine the reason she stayed in what we considered to be an abusive relationship. Not that he physically abused her because with 3 brothers and 5 sisters that was not going to go unchecked. But what we observed was the verbal abuse. He was always putting her down. When he said jump she would.

Even during all of what he put her through she never said an evil word about him to any of us. We had a great dislike for him. So much so that when our family heard he was terminally ill with cancer we didn't show any sorrowful emotions.

The accident that left her car smashed up like an accordion didn't take her out. A massive brain aneurism didn't take her out but it took something from her. She was not her same enthusiastic self after that. She even survived a grand mal seizure in the middle of the Atlantic Ocean thanks to our niece who single handedly lifted her up out of the water and carried her to shore.

We have also heard this saying; that someone may have died from a broken heart. Although not medically proven our family concluded that once she realized her husband...the man she had been attached and committed to for so long was dead, she died too...from a broken heart.

Rest in Peace Marie
"I will always love you."

Song of Praise
"If anybody asks you where I'm going, soon,
Tell them for me
I'm going UP yonder to be with my Lord."
Tramaine Hawkins

Personal Reflections

Chapter Two
Gloria

As far back as high school Gloria had always been a part of my life. We cut classes together, partied, went to concerts and got high together. I left North Carolina in 1986 in quest for a new life in California. I wanted to say goodbye to her but she was nowhere to be found.

When I returned home in 1990 I wanted to witness to her about how God had changed my life. My family and friends would tell me that she could be seen hanging out on the block in the Smith Homes projects. I would drive by there and various other places that we used to hang out or where she may have lived at one time or another looking for a family member or someone who could tell me of her where a bouts. The answer was always the same until around 2006. Thank you, Jesus for saving my friend. I love you Gloria.

Gloria. From the time I was 10 years old I had a dream of how my life was going to be. I loved school and always participated in extracurricular activities. My grandmother took me and my siblings to church. She taught us about God to the best of her ability but I didn't have a clue. Like most teenagers at 15, I thought I was grown.
I became sexually active and at the age of 16, I was *"in love"* and pregnant by a married man. I thought he was my world. When my mother found out she took me to have an abortion.

In spite of that I continued to see him and got pregnant again at the age of 17. I kept this baby and still managed to graduate from high school. I got pregnant again and had a second abortion.

I went on to live what I thought was a fairytale life. Even though my daughter's father was someone else's husband he still took care of us. This allowed me to work and complete one year of college. I always took pride in my appearance. People always told me how beautiful I was so I took care to nurture that part of my being. At the age of 20 I lost my left leg to bone cancer.

Of course that was devastating. I did not know how to deal with being an amputee at such a young age. When I woke up from the removal of my leg I had an artificial one. It was very uncomfortable and it really didn't bother me until I was released from the hospital and had to re-enter into society. After losing my leg I felt like my life was over. I felt embarrassed and ashamed walking around on one leg. I was picked on and made fun of by children and adults alike.

I later received a prosthetic leg with a covering that I wore for about two years. By this time I was heavily addicted to drugs so much so that when my leg broke I did not get it fixed. I hobbled around on crutches for about fifteen years.

Since I did not know the bible I had no moral compass. With everything I was going through drugs became a way of life for me. I began to like the marijuana I was introduced to in high school more and more because it helped me escape from self-inflicted mental abuse, anger and low self-esteem. Smoking weed led to taking acid, snorting cocaine and when the "white ghost" crack cocaine was introduced to me it soon became the love of my life.

The drugs comforted me and helped me to escape the pain I was feeling from the loss of my leg. From that point on I was on one big never ending rollercoaster ride that lasted 30 years. By the time my friend came back from California in search of me I was really out there. I had my own place but I had no electricity and I stored what little provisions I had outside in a cooler. When she got a chance to see me she told me about Jesus Christ. I heard her but it just didn't make any sense to me (I Corinthians 1:18). Seeing her and how well she was doing...it was a great feeling. I wanted what I saw in her but it seemed beyond my reach.

My friend shared II Corinthians 5:17 with me. She told me salvation was free and she challenged me to ask God, the Lord Jesus Christ to reveal Himself to me (Ephesians 2:8). I did many times and every time the devil attacked me even harder because I really was not ready.

I do not have enough fingers and toes to count the number of times I went to jail. I would even go to jail with a crack pipe hid in a certain part of my body. While I was locked up I couldn't wait to get out so that I could return to the same old people, places and things I was familiar with. Just imagine a one-legged, crack-head prostitute hanging on the block looking for a john, a fix, somebody to con or rip-off. I was my own worst enemy because many of my actions caused me to be victimized as well.

I went to prison 3 times. The third and final time I served 14 months. That's when I finally felt sick and tired of being incarcerated. Let me tell you... jail house salvation is real. The messages I was hearing about Jesus began to sink in. I began to develop a personal relationship with my heavenly father. I remember lying on my bed in a small prison cell one Saturday evening around 5 pm. I was listening to the word of God on the radio and when I opened my mouth to give him a praise the spirit of God moved on me and an utterance of tongues came forth (I Corinthians 14:2). I was so amazed that I was found worthy for God to visit me right where I was. Thank you, Jesus.

Upon my release I was supposed to catch the bus at 9:00 am

but the officer who was driving lived right there in the city of Raleigh and could not find the bus station. I was taken back to the facility until 2 pm. During that wait time God used the same correctional officer who had witnessed to me throughout my sentence. She ministered and prophesied to me about what God had for me (Jeremiah 29:11) and that I would never come back to that place again. She was correct. I never went back to prison.

After I got home I did not have the desire to indulge in drug use again. Nor did I want to go to the same places or see the same people I used to hang out with. That's when I realized I was free (John 8:36).

> *"If the Son therefore shall make you free, ye shall be free indeed."*
> **John 8:36**

When I did go out into the world the devil tried to set me up. I was attacked by a drug dealer who tried to plant crack on me but God gave me the victory in that situation and I was able to get away.

During my addiction I had two other children now young adults. God had placed a Christian woman in my daughter's life who served as a mother figure for her before He delivered me. Her name was Miss Erica. She was always there for my daughter. Her hair was always pretty and she always gave props to her beautician Miss Shirley. Months went by before I actually got a chance to meet Miss Shirley for myself.

Becoming a new creature in Christ was a process. One morning when I was really going through I walked into Miss

Shirley's beauty shop and there were angels all over the place. It felt like a safe haven for me. I was struggling with trying to live a new life, be normal but the world was beating me down. My son was being rebellious and I saw my past life being relived through him. He was running the streets and getting into trouble with the law. I became depressed because it seemed like there was nothing I could do to stop him.

From that day forward my life has never been the same. Miss Shirley became my angel. She ministered the word of God to me, prayed with me and held my hands for months until Christ was totally formed in me. She did my hair on a regular basis without charging, trusted me with a key to her shop and eventually purchased a car for me. She was an answer to my prayers until God sent my husband to me
(I Corinthians 7:2).

If there was one scripture that I could apply to my situation it would be Romans 8:28. When the bible says *"all things work together for the good of those who love the Lord and are called according to his purpose."* I can truly say that my drug use and everything that came with it worked for my good because I accepted Jesus Christ as my Lord and Savior while I was locked up in prison.

God does answer prayer and somebody was always praying for me. I was scared to leave prison but the Lord Jesus Christ had saved and delivered me before I stepped foot out of the prison gates.

There was a time in my life when I thought drugs were the best thing that ever happened to me but having a personal relationship with the Lord Jesus is truly the best thing that ever happened to me. He replaced my hatred and low self-esteem with the fruit of the spirit (Galatians 5:22-23).

That's why I always have praise in my heart because when the devil wanted to kill me God said no (John10:10).

Everything the devil stole from me God gave it all back and then some (Isaiah 61:7). He blessed me with a wonderful husband who not only ministers the word of God but he teaches and ministers to me personally.

My first born daughter is now 37 years old. God has truly blessed her with a wonderful husband, a family and a career. I had lost custody of my son and daughter when they were younger but thanks to God I got them back several years ago. There was a time when...if someone asked me who their father was I would have been ashamed to say I did not know. But now that I am a new creature in Christ Jesus I am not ashamed of my past (Romans 8:1).

I have been drug-free for eight years. This past November 2013, I was married one year. I have a new prosthesis that I take care of and no one would ever know that it's not my real leg. God changed me from the inside out and a lot of people don't recognize the new me (Psalm 149:4). I am a beautiful woman and I love my life. It was all a part of His plan. To God be the glory.

My Song of Praise
"He saw the best in me when everyone else around could only see the worst in me."
Pastor Marvin Sapp

Scripture References

I Corinthians 1:18 - For the preaching of the cross is to them that perish foolishness; but unto us which are saved it is the power of God.

II Corinthians 5:17 - Therefore if any man be in Christ, he is a new creature: old things are pasted away; behold, all things are become new.

Ephesians 2:8 - For by grace are ye saved through faith; and that not of yourselves: *it is* the gift of God:

I Corinthians 14:2 - For he that speaketh in an unknown tongue speaketh not unto men, but unto God:

Jeremiah 29:11 - For I know the thoughts that I think toward you, saith the Lord, thoughts of peace and not of evil, to give you an expected end.

John 8:36 - If the son of man therefore shall make you free, ye shall be free indeed.

I Corinthians 7:2 - Nevertheless, to avoid fornication, let every man have his own wife, and let every woman have her own husband.

Galatians 5:22, 23 - But the fruit of the Spirit is love, joy, peace, longsuffering, gentleness, goodness, faith, (23) - Meekness, temperance: against such is no law,

John10:10 - The thief cometh not, but for to steal, and to kill, and to destroy: I am come that they might have life, and that they might have it more abundantly.

Isaiah 61:7 - For your shame *ye shall have* double.

Romans 8:1- There is therefore now no condemnation to them which are in Christ Jesus, who walk not after the flesh, but after the Spirit.

Psalm 149:4 - For the Lord taketh pleasure in his people: he will beautify the meek with salvation.

Personal Reflections

Chapter Three
Betty

Betty and I met in 1981 at Morgan and Sons Poultry Company while cutting livers from the chickens as they sped past us hanging upside down on the assembly line. We immediately became friends and began carpooling to work. On numerous mornings we would pass truckloads of live chickens in route to the plant knowing that by the end of the day we would pass those same chickens dead, boxed in ice and on their way to the supermarket by our hands. Even though we now live thousands of miles apart distance has only cemented our friendship. I love you Betty.

Betty. I came from a large family, born third from the last of 18 children. We grew up in a small country town in North Carolina. By the time I was 19, I was pregnant with my first child. Back then having children out of wedlock was unacceptable. My father was very angry with me which made it unbearable for me to stay in my parent's house so I left. Although my oldest sister sought me out and brought me back home my father never made me feel welcome.

When my daughter was nearly a year old I met and married Bob a much older man. Not that I really loved him but because he was a means of escape from my parent's house. As the years went by Bob began to drink excessively at home and at work. Despite his drinking and the turmoil in our relationship he always took care of our four children.

As time went by Bob began to bring his male co-workers home to hang out.

They would drink alcohol late into the night. One man in particular would hit on me. He had also served time in prison for murder. He carried a handgun and used it to persuade me to be with him. Ultimately he would buy alcohol to intoxicate my husband so that he could take advantage of me. I was too afraid to tell anyone and when I tried to convey my fears to Bob he only dismissed my concerns, boasting that *he* was not afraid of this man.

One night in the midst of their drinking they got into a physical altercation. Bob was too drunk to really know what was going on. So I took matters into my own hands and did what I had to do to protect my family. I shot him. Thank God he didn't die. I prayed that God would help me avoid having to go to jail or get any prison time. He answered my prayers. However I was put on probation for five years.

It was not until much later...Bob informed me that he was aware of this man's advances towards me. I couldn't believe he knew and chose not to do anything about it. We were together for a total of 13 years before separating. Even though my life had been chaotic I held on to my faith in the true and living God as I trained my children in the way they should go (Proverbs 22:6).

A short time after my separation from Bob I met and began dating James a recently discharged Army veteran. We developed a very nice relationship and I felt comfortable enough to move in with him when he asked me to. We did good for a while until my four children ages 8-14 years old moved in with us.

He began to complain about everything from a piece of paper on the floor to a dish left in the sink. He was especially jealous of the relationship I had with my oldest daughter. Eventually I discovered that he too was an alcoholic. I would find empty bottles stashed around the house.

One day after working a double shift I came home to find him passed out on the sofa. He reeked of alcohol. I got up the next morning, took a shower and went back to work. When I came home he accused me of staying out all night with another man. Not only that but he accused me of meeting someone at church or even at my mother's house. I stopped visiting my mom as often as I would have liked to because we would always end up arguing. Even then I kept going to church with my children. I knew God was protecting us (Psalm 91:11).

Once when he was angry with me he took it out on my daughter and hit her. In an attempt to defend himself he called the police to have us removed from his premises. I called the police on him as well to report that he had been abusive towards my child. He was arrested and taken to jail. That was my way of escape (I Corinthians 10:13). I left and never returned.

It seemed like I didn't know how to exist without a man in my life. So when Winston a handy man was doing repair work at a rental house I lived in we started talking and as time went by we began dating. He was really nice...at first.

He would do all the things a woman wanted a man to do. Like send flowers and dedicate love songs to me on the radio. I developed a trust in him and when he asked me to relocate to his hometown in another state I did. We lived with his family members and I was able to find employment. Soon after that he became very abusive. One night he beat me so bad his brother intervened to make him stop.

Winston had promised me that once his ailing mother passed away we would move back to North Carolina. Although he kept his word things didn't get any better in fact thy got worse. He would beat me for no reason at all. I would cover up the bruises on my arms to hide them from my children. I discovered that not only was he drinking alcohol but he was using drugs as well.

We were both employed and depositing our monies into a joint bank account. I was getting money out and writing checks for household expenses. He was getting money out and writing checks to his drug dealer. Soon the checks began to bounce.

Even while I was going through with Winston the one thing that sustained me was my faith in God and attending church. I remember my mother always said God would take care of us (Psalm 46:1) and although I was close in location to my family that didn't stop the beatings.

I will always remember a Thanksgiving in 1990. Our oven was not working so I brought dinner home from a restaurant. He didn't want that so he threw it in the garbage can. He beat me once again then made me have sex with him. We went to bed hungry that night. I felt like I had nothing to be thankful for. I cried out to God for Him to deliver me from the hands of this evil man and he did (Psalm 34:6). Several days later we broke up.

Even though I only had a 12th grade education God always blessed me with employment. Later on I met Brian when I was working at a motel. We got acquainted and dated for a while. I told my girlfriend Mae that something wasn't right about him. When I started to withdraw from him he noticed and plotted to end my life.

I don't know what it was about me that always attracted the wrong kind of men. We were riding in the country one day when for no apparent reason he hit me in my face. He drove further and further into the unknown as darkness began to set in. He threatened to leave me in the wilderness. I immediately began to think of how I could escape.

When Brian pulled up to a stop sign I jumped out of the car and ran into the woods. I remembered what I had heard or read somewhere; if you are in the woods follow the sounds of the traffic. Feeling like some woman in a lifetime movie I traveled through the woods until I spotted a trailer with the lights on. I knocked on the door. A man and woman saw I was in trouble and let me in. They drove me to my sister's house. After that night I never saw that fool again. I later found out that he was using cocaine.

Bob, James, Winston, Brian, now Frank. We worked at the same housing development. Several weeks passed before he started talking to me. After so many negative experiences with men I did not want to rush into another relationship. I took my time and observed his character and personality. Eventually we started dating. He introduced me to his adult children and I developed a good relationship with most of them.

We decided to live together in sin... but I continued attending church on a regular basis taking his young granddaughter Brittany with me. I would always ask Frank to go and he would always say no. One day I believe the spirit of God told me to stop asking him to go so I did. God also revealed to me that he was a drug dealer. I prayed that God would deliver him and as his clientele began to fade I could see the hand of God moving in answer to my prayers (I John 5:14-15). A year and a half later we got married (Hebrews 13:4).

As the years passed Frank's health began to fail. He had a chronic history of diabetes when I met him. It was getting harder and harder to manage. Then his kidneys began to fail so he had to go on dialysis. After about a year of that his doctor called me into his office and informed me that my husband no longer wanted to continue his treatment.

I didn't know how to process that news. When I came to myself that evening my children had been called to pick me up and take me home. In between praying that God would help me to accept my husband's decision all I could think of was the many years I had wasted in crazy abusive relationships. Now to finally meet a good man, a man who grew to believe in and serve the same God as I did...just to see him suffer was painful.

Three years before this I had been diagnosed with breast cancer but it was now in remission. Around the same time that Frank was going through I started experiencing pain in the lower right side of my stomach. I continued in prayer asking God to let me be able to take care of my husband. He answered that prayer request as well.

Frank did die from his illness. Three months later I was diagnosed with colon cancer, a diagnosis I had made myself. Prior to getting sick this time God had called me to preach. I had known for a long time that this was my calling but like Jonah I chose to run (Jonah 1:1-3). I tried to appease God by becoming a deaconess and an usher but I knew the entire time what I was supposed to be doing. It got so bad I couldn't sleep at night. I finally said, "yes Lord, not my will but *your* will be done."

A few weeks later I talked to my pastor about being called to preach. He said he knew all along but was just waiting for me to come to him. I thank God for keeping me, for delivering me, for healing me and for not giving up on me (Psalm 34:19).

> *"Many are the afflictions of the righteous:
> but the Lord delivereth
> him out of them all."*
> Psalm 34:19

When I was diagnosed with colon cancer in 2011, I had just found out that my oldest grandson was expecting my first great-grandchild. Also, my oldest son was getting ready to graduate with his degree as a medical assistant. I asked God to let me live to see the birth of my first great-grandchild and my son's graduation.

While I was going through treatment my best friend came home from California. During her visit I was scheduled to have a chemo treatment. My friend asked if she could come with me. Of course my response was yes. It made me feel so good to be blessed with a friend like her.

Once again God answered my prayers (James 5:16b). He blessed me to see my son's graduation and the birth of my great-granddaughter. There was also one more thing I'd always wanted to do. That was to visit my friend in California. In 2012 God made a way for me, my daughter and my sister to fly to California for a visit. We had a wonderful time.

I am now an ordained minister. I love preaching the gospel and giving my testimony about what God can do if you only trust and believe in Him. I will always give God the praise and the glory. Without Him in my life I wouldn't be here today. No matter what happens in your life always keep your hand in God's hand. He will see you through it all. ***Amen.***

My Song of Praise
"After you've done all you can, you just stand."
Pastor Donnie McClurkin

Scripture References

Proverbs 22:6 – Train up a child in the way he should go, And when he is old he will not depart from it.

Psalm 91:11 – For he shall give his angels charge over thee, to keep thee in all thy ways.

I Corinthians 10:13 – There hath no temptation taken you but such as is common to man: but God *is* faithful, who will not suffer you to be tempted above that ye are able; but will with the temptation also make a way to escape, that ye may be able to bear *it*.

Psalm 46:1 – God *is* our refuge and strength, a very present help in trouble.

Psalm 34:6 – This poor man cried, and the Lord heard *him*, and saved him out of all his troubles.

I John 5:14-15 – And this is the confidence that we have in him, that, if we ask any thing according to his will, he heareth us: (15) And if we know that he hear us, whatsoever we ask, we know that we have the petitions that we desired of him.

Hebrews 13:4a – Marriage is honorable in all, and the bed undefiled:

Jonah 1:1 -3 – Now the word of the Lord came unto Jonah the son of Amittai, saying, (2) Arise, go to Nineveh, that great city, and cry against it; for their wickedness is come up before me. (3) But Jonah rose up to flee unto Tarshish from the presence of the Lord,

Psalms 34:19 – Many are the afflictions of the righteous: but the LORD delivereth him out of them all.

James 5:16b – The effectual fervent prayer of a righteous man availeth much.

Personal Reflections

Chapter Four
Margo

In 1986 when I relocated to California with my four year old son, one of the first women I met was Margo. She and her husband Ronald had a son the same age as my son. Our families immediately connected and we became sisters and friends for life. Twenty eight years later we both acknowledge that we still have a relationship that exist even though we seldom see each other, text or talk daily on the phone. We know that our mutual love, respect, care and concern will always be intact no matter what occurs in our lives. Margo and her husband shared their story together. Thank you both. Thank you, Margo for always being consistent. I love you and my brother Ron.

Margo. I was born in Pittsburg Pennsylvania but was raised in Chicago Illinois. When I was a teenager I showed a strong interest in fashion and at 14, I attended the Sa-Mar Sewing Center for Dress design. At age 17, I attended the John Robert Powers Modeling School. At age 18, I graduated from Percy L. Julian High School in Chicago. Afterwards I joined the US Army. While in the military I met and married my husband Ronald Harper at the 9th Avenue Chapel in Fort Ord, California. In 1979 we had our first child, a boy, born in Frankfurt Germany.

The youngest of three children I was raised with both parents in the home and we attended church as Methodist. When I got older I practiced the Baptist faith before embracing the Church of God in Christ doctrine. My husband was introduced to the Baptist faith as a child by his grandmother who took him to church in Louisiana. During our pre-marital counseling we both agreed that practicing our faith would be an essential part of our union (Ecclesiastes 4:12).

My interest in fashion and beauty continued when I enrolled in the Aladdin Beauty College while stationed in Lawton, Oklahoma. Being in the military we moved around a lot. We eventually decided to make our home in Oakland California where we became long time members of Acts Full Gospel Church of God in Christ. I served as an usher, marriage and bible study teacher for the youth ministry and a SWAT (Spreading the Word Across Town) team member.
In 1985 I joined the California Army National Guard where I was a Personnel Records Specialist. In 1988 I gave birth to our second child a girl.

Always pursuing a pathway to a career I attended the Chabot College for Dental Radiography and the Oakland Dental and Medical College where I received certificates in Dental Assisting, X-Ray techniques and CPR.

In 1992 we said good-bye to all of our church family and friends and moved back to Chicago. While there I attended Prairie State College. In 1994 we moved back to California. Where once again I enrolled in a course for the Essentials of Anesthesia as an emerging passion for the medical field lead to completing courses for a degree in Health Science from the College of Alameda while continuing to study and learn medical terminology at the San Francisco VA Medical Center. I am currently certified by the American Society of Anesthesia Technologist and Technicians with the California State Board.

Always a petite sized woman I vowed early in life to take care of and preserve my "body temple" as a long standing jazzercise and YMCA member. I eat healthy and have made physical fitness a part of my daily life. I am presently a member of the Vegetarian Society and the Vegan One Club an organization that strives to raise public awareness about healthier food choices through direct social outreach designed to empower people on how to make positive choices when it comes to food consumption.

As you can see I have lead an on point focused and disciplined life...but none of that stopped my husband from **cheating** on me. **HE CHEATED. He cheated** on me with someone in the church. And allegedly a child was conceived. That's why we left our church family and friends in 1992. The hint of a scandal was embarrassing for us as leaders in the church. We left to save face, to try to save our marriage and to shield our two young children.

I hated him for what he did to me, to us to our family. Of course my flesh wanted to respond in an ungodly way. I literally wanted to scratch his eyes out (Ephesians 4:26).

All throughout my relationship with God...He had always showed me things to come (John 16:13). It took Ronald's uncle Joe to give me some insight into the generational curse of womanizing that yet plagued my husband.

All the many times uncle Joe had been telling me about his struggles with women and infidelity as a teenage boy into adulthood was intended to fore-warn me about what was to come with his nephew. So when my husband's womanizing came full circle I couldn't get that angry because in hindsight God had already given me a glimpse into the future.

But still... in my flesh I had to react like a sister. I know vengeance belongs to the Lord (Romans 12:19b) but I had to release my anger and I did just that for many, many, many days. For hours without end I let him have it.

Ronald Because of my wife's strong faith in God and the Lord's mercy and grace, as well as her commitment to our family, our marital vows and her confidence in me she was willing to forgive me for my past indiscretions.

Forgiveness (Ephesians 4:32) through the word of God was essential in order for us to move past all the hurt, anger, disappointment and shame I imposed on my wife in order for us to be where we are 36 years later. I realized that the steps to forgiveness followed the systematic process of a revival. In that there was a breaking down of emotions and a building up of the same. I was willing to do whatever it took because I wanted to save my marriage. Rebuilding trust continues to be an ongoing process in our marriage.

Margo Since we began our relationship as friends even when it seemed like the love was gone I still liked Ronald as a friend. Friends take the good, the bad and the ugly (Proverbs 17:17). There was many a time when our friendship carried our relationship. We had mutually agreed that if we ever went our separate ways and the marriage was dissolved we would still remain friends.

However, there did come a time when I felt like we needed to exist under separate roofs. I finally got fed up with his ongoing imbalances and crazy choices. Throughout the course of our marriage we had been to numerous counseling sessions. One in particular concluded that we would try separation as an option before filing for divorce. So we did.

I waited until Ronald was away at school in Little Rock Arkansas to move out (I Corinthians 14:33). I moved to an apartment, worked two jobs to support myself and for the first time in my adult life I had to pay rent. Prior to that, my husband had always provided for me and our children. He continued to assist us financially even when we were separated.

As time went on our oldest son completed Junior College and needed our parental support financially in order to transfer to UC Davis. Therefore it became economically sound for both parents to be under the same roof. I gave up my place and moved in with Ronald not as husband and wife but as roommates so that we could contribute to our son's college education. He had his space and I had my space. Ronald was happy to let me come back. He never wanted his wife to leave. He did not believe in divorce because he came from a broken home.

Ronald left for a year and a half to serve his country in Iraq. Because I genuinely loved him as a person once he returned we decided to see if we could rekindle this love connection. I am ever so grateful to God for his safe return (Psalm 136:1).

Over the years my trust in him has **not** been totally restored. Even today 2/4/2014 I trust him as far as I can see him. But I can accept his personality and the issues that come with him. After all we have been married 36 years. I have learned to take the good with the bad and the bitter with the sweet.

Throughout our marriage as parents I constantly prayed over our children, especially the male child (married 6 years to a beautiful young lady, together they have 2 sons). I would anoint him with oil when he was asleep so that he would not continue on with this legacy of male infidelity. I desperately wanted our son to be the one to break the generational curse of infidelity.

On my son's 23rd birthday he dictated the words to express how he felt as his wife penned them on paper. She wrote *"Thank you ma for making the sacrifice to stay with my dad even though you wanted to leave."* I really appreciated my son's expression of love and respect for me. In hindsight he is why I stayed.

Ronald I have learned how to get the victory over myself during my decision making process. Especially when my flesh wants to do what I want it to do. When that occurs I increase my study in the word of God to see how my actions grieve a holy God. I have to also consider the sacrifice God made for me and that the power of God is able to keep me from falling (Jude 1:24).

> **"Now unto him that is able**
> **to keep you from falling,"**
> **Jude 1:24**

I thank God for my wife standing by me. She worked with me through my adolescence exemplifying the love of God in 1 Corinthians 13 known as the love chapter.

She recently bought *me* a new car. I asked her to give me a year after working at my new career so that I could give her whatever she wanted. She deserves not just material things but she deserves all of my love, respect and honor. I want her to be able to trust me 100%. She's my friend and my lover. I want us to enjoy each other. I sincerely love my wife (Ephesians 5:25).

Margo. My mother was hurt by all the things my husband had done to me. I had the chance to have a heart to heart talk with her during an eight hour flight over the Atlantic Ocean in route to Europe for our mother and daughter vacation. I didn't know at that time that she was coming to the end of her life. However before she passed away she told me how much she respected my decision to stay in my marriage and she was glad that I did not let her opinions influence my decisions to stay. I always consulted my God who always overrode my decision to leave (Proverbs 3:5, 6). Even though I felt like my mother transitioned too soon she knew in her heart that I was happy.

My Song of Praise
"God has smiled on me. He has set me free."
Reverend James Cleveland

Scripture References

Ecclesiastes 4:12 – And if one prevail against him, two shall withstand him; and a threefold cord is not quickly broken.

Ephesians 4:26, 27 – Be ye angry, and sin not: let not the sun go down on your wrath: Neither give place to the devil.

John 16:13 – Howbeit when he, the Spirit of truth, is come, he will guide you into all truth: for he shall not speak of himself; but whatsoever he shall hear, *that* shall he speak: and he will show you things to come.

Romans 12:19b – for it is written, Vengeance is mine; I will repay, saith the Lord.

Ephesians 4:32 – And be ye kind one to another, tenderhearted, forgiving one another, even as God for Christ's sake hath forgiven you.

Proverbs 17:17 – A friend loveth at all times, and a brother is born for adversity.

I Corinthians 14:33 – For God is not *the author* of confusion, but of peace, as in all churches of the saints.

Psalm 136:1 – O give thanks unto the LORD; *for he is* good: for his mercy *endureth* forever.

Jude 1:24 – Now unto him that is able to keep you from falling, and to present *you f*aultless before the presence of his glory with exceeding joy.

I Corinthians 13: 4 – Charity (love) suffereth long, *and* is kind; charity envieth not; charity vaunteth not itself, is not puffed up.

Ephesians 5:25 – Husbands, love your wives, even as Christ also loved the church, and gave himself for it;

Proverbs 3:5, 6 – Trust in the Lord with all thine heart; and lean not unto thine own understanding. (6) In thy ways acknowledge him, and he shall direct thy paths.

Personal Reflections

Chapter Five
Juanita

I met Juanita at the church we attended together for nearly twenty years. It was love at first sight. Not only did I fall in love with her but I fell in love with her sisters Lois, Lytania their brother Ira and their mother. She had two other sisters that I briefly knew. Her siblings reminded me of my own family in that there were 6 girls and 3 boys who each had distinct personalities but all fit together like a hand in a glove.

Juanita could be seen on Sundays ministering to the hearing impaired using sign language during our church services. She did so with the same grace and elegance that she worshipped and walked in. When my husband and I became homeowners in 1992 she was one of the sisters who helped my husband surprise me with a house warming fellowship. I will always remember that. Thank you, Juanita. I love you.

Juanita. I was born in Oakland California, the seventh of 8 siblings, 6 girls and 2 boys. I became pregnant my junior year by my high school sweetheart and gave birth to twin girls on October 14, 1974. I was determined not to let my status as a new and unwed mother deter me from completing my high school education. With the support of my family I graduated and walked across the stage with the class of 1975. After high school I worked part time at Laney College while also attending classes. Unfortunately my dad passed away the same year my twin daughters were born.

I had the opportunity to attend the East Bay Skills Center. During my training there I tested far better than any other attendees and was hired by Pacific Bell (Pac Bell) Telephone Company in 1980. As a single mother and woman raising my twins men would come and go but I never let them get close to my girls. I was and still am very protective of them.

One of the benefits of working for Pac Bell was 100% tuition assistance. I took advantage of the opportunity to pursue my dream of going to college and began attending the University of Phoenix and Holy Names College. But I made the mistake of dropping out before completing my education.

I learned about the Lord Jesus Christ at an early age. Like most people when I got old enough I departed from God. I began living my life doing things my way (Proverbs 14:12). Although I knew about the Lord I did not have a personal relationship with him and neither did I want one. I had convinced myself that I enjoyed the night life, the clubbing, the drinking and the drugs because it made me feel good. In reality I was covering up the loneliness, the hurt, pain and disappointments I was experiencing as well as the emotional pain I allowed others to inflict on me.

God used a sister at the church I now attend to witness to me. We were co-workers at Pac Bell and she was relentless. She finally wore me down. I gave in and accepted an invitation to attend a revival, thinking if I went she would leave me alone. I believe that God began to deal with me during those services. I wanted more.

I rededicated my life to the Lord Jesus Christ and began attending foundation classes offered by the church for people who needed a deeper understanding of who Jesus is before they became members. That was nearly 26 years ago and I have been a member of Acts Full Gospel (COGIC) Church of God in Christ since then. The sister God used to witness to me was the founding first lady who has since gone home to be with the Lord.

I began to really study and learn the word of God (II Timothy 2:15). I was excited for the first time in a long time and I wanted to learn more and more about the Lord Jesus Christ. When I read the bible it was as if God was speaking directly to me and He was.

As time went on I developed a relationship with a young man I met at Radio Shack. After a few months of getting acquainted we decided to become a couple and he moved in with me and my daughters in our two bedroom apartment. Eventually we were going to be married. I didn't know that this was not pleasing in the sight of God.

Since I didn't know I dismissed Relationships 101; never move a man into your home when children are involved. Because if it doesn't work out children are sometimes left to feel abandoned or the person may be more interested in your children than in you in an ungodly way.

During the planning of our wedding I picked out the beautiful marquis diamond that was to be placed in a setting. I had purchased the finest fabrics the designer would use for my dress as well as for the bridesmaids. I had a wedding coordinator, flower girls and groomsmen. I had a beautiful ivory photo album made and my fiancee who was a graphics designer was creating our invitations. How wonderful right? So I thought because while I continued to go to church with my girls he did not attend with us.

One Sunday my Pastor preached a sermon outlining what fornication was. I had no idea that I was living in that sin (I Corinthians 6:18). I invited my fiancée to come to church to hear the word preached in terms that we could totally understand several times. One Sunday he surprised me and finally said yes. I was hallelujah happy. However we continued to live in sin until conviction came upon me and I asked him to move out until our wedding date. Reluctantly he agreed and moved out.

It felt liberating to be delivered from alcohol, drugs, clubbing *and* fornication. Finally I was in a great place in my life. In love with the man of my dreams, children were obedient, the job was good and I had God on my side. What could go wrong?

As time went on things began to change. My fiancée began to change. He became distant, harsh and uncaring towards me. That's when I realized there was someone else. But I didn't know who. Surprisingly one night at church as I was walking to my car after attending a women's meeting I saw him walking with another woman from church. When they looked up and saw me we were all speechless. How dare he? How could she? My entire world stood still.

I managed to speak. I managed to make it to my car. I managed to unlock and get in my car as she got in the truck with him. The same truck I used to ride in. My heart sank. I cried all the way home. When I got home I fell to my knees. I prayed and cried myself to sleep. In the middle of the night I woke up questioning why. Why would he get involved in another relationship when we were engaged to be married? Why did this sister in the church do this knowing we were a couple? Everybody at church knew we were engaged to be married. Why Lord why?

The truth had been revealed (I Corinthians 4:5). They no longer had to sneak around. I had so many raw emotions. I felt rejected, betrayed, broken hearted, angry, bitter, resentful and most of all I felt like being violent. In my younger years I had a serious, problem with my temper. Now that I am a new creature in Christ Jesus that old woman wanted to resurrect (I Corinthians 5:17).

Thank God for the many prayers of the righteous. I never said a mumbling word even though my ex taunted me with his new fiancée. It felt like Peninnah did Hannah when she went into the temple to pray (1 Samuel 1:2, 7). I kept praising the Lord with my broken hearted self.

Every time the church doors opened I was there. My Pastor and first lady really encouraged me with the word of God. Oftentimes people think the grass is greener on the other side, but it merely means there is a higher water bill. I kept going to church with my children and I kept growing in the word. I knew that in God's time he would heal me from the hurt and pain I had to endure. The two of them eventually got married as he placed the diamond on her finger that I had picked out and... and we all continued to attend the same church (Hebrews 10:25).

God is a healer (Psalm 107:20). One day I suddenly realized that I had let that thing go. There were a lot of people angry and wanted the world's justice for me. Thank God I did not act on those actions neither did I allow anyone else to. After that ordeal I knew I was saved. Thank the Lord Jesus for changing me and giving me a new heart.

> *"He sent his word, and healed them,*
> *and delivered them*
> *from their destructions."*
> **Psalm 107:20**

One Sunday morning during my devotion time a song came on the radio, *He's Preparing Me*, by Reverend Darryl Coley. All of a sudden I sat straight up and listened to the words. It was as if God Himself was speaking directly to me. This was the beginning of a new relationship with the new me. The song went on to say: *"He's preparing me for something I cannot handle right now. He's making me ready just because He cares. He's providing me with what I'll need to carry out the next matter in my life."*

I purchased this piece of music in cassette form and played it day in and day out. Several weeks went by when I suddenly realized that the pain was gone. My heart did not ache anymore. The tears had dried up (Psalm 30:5b). I don't know when it actually happened but I do know that it was gone. So much so that I was able to practice the scripture that says pray for your enemies (Matthew 5:44). Not only did I speak to them both but I prayed for them as well. Hallelujah! Thank you Lord Jesus. To God be the glory for the things He has done.

The Bible says occupy till Jesus comes (Luke 19:13). That's exactly what I did. I became active in the signing ministry and became department head for the singles ministry. Every time the church doors opened I was there.

There was a brother at the church who had a limousine service. I took it upon myself to inquire about his fees which opened the door for us to have many conversations. He eventually asked me out for dinner. We met at a local restaurant in Jack London Square. It was a very nice evening.

I listened intently as this man shared his entire life story with me. After leaving the restaurant we went our separate ways. I thought to myself he would be quite a catch; tall, dark and handsome. As well as being a perfect gentleman and a Godly man with gainful employment. Within a few minutes of leaving his presence it hit me like a ton of bricks right in the pit of my stomach...this brother was interested enough in me to want to marry me.

Oh my God!! That's all I kept saying on my way home. I knew from that moment on what his intentions would be so I immediately began praying for guidance (Proverbs 3:5-6).

When he proposed my answer was yes. I didn't have to say wait brother I need to pray about it or I'll get back to you. I had already received my confirmations and I knew without a shadow of a doubt that he was to be my husband
(I Thessalonians 5:21).

We were united in holy matrimony at Acts Full Gospel COGIC on September 17, 1997. It was a beautiful wedding. There were 12 bridesmaids and 12 groomsmen, one flower girl and ring bearer, two psalmists and three signers for the hearing impaired. My uncle walked me down that long church aisle in the absence of my beloved dad. It seemed to take forever and a day. But we made it. Our reception was at Hs Lordships in Berkeley.

This was one of the brightest days of my life. We were so happy in love. It seemed like the world was our oyster. My new husband was my king and I was his queen we shared many dreams. Because of the nature of my husband's business we did not go away for a honeymoon. We just spent a few days in a local hotel suite. And then life returned back to normal.

My husband continued with his limousine business and I continued with my Mary Kay in addition to my employment in San Francisco at the Wells Fargo Corporate office. Hence finances were booming and house hunting was under way. The very first home we looked at my spirit became troubled and I didn't know why. As life went on our marital relationship grew stronger and then we experienced a major blow.

My husband called me one day feeling terrible. I rushed home prayed with him and believed God for his healing. However as time went on he continued to experience excruciating pain. We immediately sought medical advice. After numerous tests the results revealed that my husband had terminal cancer and there was nothing that could be done. I was speechless as the doctor went on to say that all he could do was make him as comfortable as possible which included setting up hospice to attend to him at our home.

I really don't remember hearing much after that. I sat down in shock as endless tears rolled down my cheeks. I cried out to God in anger how could you do this to me? I waited a long time for my Mr. Right and now you are taking him from me. You blessed me with this wonderful man of God I know that you did. I've only had him for two and a half years and now you are taking him away.

I could not believe the news we had just received. During the ride home I was silent as my husband tried to console me. Even though my husband was a mighty man of God it was as if he had accepted the doctor's prognosis while at the same time believing the Lord's report that he was healed (Isaiah 53:1).

His health started to deteriorate more and more right in front of my very eyes. His doctor appointments increased as the pain intensified. In the midst of all of that he still wanted to make it out to the house of prayer. Even if it meant he had to enter into the house of prayer in a wheelchair.

The saints ministered to us with their prayers and encouraging words. Like the unselfish man my husband was he requested that prayers would be offered up for me. WOW! What a mighty man of God. On December 9, 1999 my husband was rushed to the hospital by ambulance. The following day the Lord fore-warned me that he was going to take him home. With several family members, saints and friends surrounding his bedside I began to pray over him.

He took his last breathe after I released him to go be with the Lord in the name of Jesus knowing that we would see each other again.

The bible says to give thanks in all things so all I could do was lift my hands and give God the glory (I Thessalonians 5:18). I knew that my husband lived the kind of life that once he was absent from his body he was with the Lord free from pain (II Corinthians 5:8).

People came from all around to pay their last respects. Some flew in while others drove. I had a tremendous amount of love and support to help me get through that difficult time. Once people started to go back to their normal lives I was left alone to begin my journey towards healing.

When it finally hit me it hit hard like a ton of bricks. I was on my way to church when I broke down and cried like a baby. Oh God! I trusted you to heal my husband. We fasted, we prayed and we believed that you would heal him.

Once I calmed down I could hear the Lord speak to me in that still small voice (I Kings 19:12). He said I did heal your husband totally and completely. I am faithful to my word. He is no longer sick, no longer in pain, no more hospice visits, no more not being able to hold down his food, no more taking all of those pills prescribed by the doctor. I healed him totally and I healed him completely. I cried again as I praised God for being faithful to His Word. Yes he did heal my husband not the way I thought it should be physically but God healed him spiritually. Thank you Lord for the time we had together in holy matrimony.

I started counseling sessions with a therapist shortly after the passing of my husband. I was still angry with God. I didn't want to pray. I didn't want to go to church. And I didn't want people praying for me. I was angry and hurt.

Approximately three months after I went into therapy I got break through. That was a good day. Until I got home and received an alarming phone call from a dear friend. She said sister I'm sorry. I didn't understand what she felt sorry about. Then there was silence on the phone. My heart pounding I said do I need to call Merced?

Merced was where my mother lived. She too was battling cancer. When I called her house my brother from Washington answered the phone. We exchanged pleasantries and when I asked to speak to my mommy there was silence on the other end of the phone. Mommy had passed comfortably in her own bed in her own home.

The following month we were cleaning out mommy's house I kept noticing bruises on my legs and arms. Because we were packing and moving around the house my sisters and I thought that maybe I was bumping into something during the process.

The next morning there were more bruises. I contacted my doctor and she suggested that I come in to have some testing done. When the doctor called with the results she wanted to make sure I was not home alone knowing that my husband and my mother had recently passed away. I assured her that I would be all right. As it turned out I was diagnosed with leukemia and it was already in its fourth and final stage. She referred me to an oncologist (cancer specialist). That was fine with me but I knew I had to call on the Thee Specialist...Jesus.

Sitting in the doctor's office I felt numb. Thank God for my sister friend who was there with me. I did not remember anything that was said. I do recall telling my physician that medically he was going to treat me but that my God was going to heal me. As fear set in I began to worry about my children, my precious grand baby and my family. But the devil is a liar and the father of lies. I began to encourage myself in the Lord. I wanted to live and not die (Psalm 118:17).

I made an entire lifestyle change beginning with my diet. Sugar, salt, processed foods and red meat had to go. I began juicing and shopping at a health food store. Due to the weakness of my immune system I had to minimize the stressors in my life as well as the interactions with large crowds in order to avoid any type of infection.

My chemotherapy treatments were very aggressive. Because the tumors were large I had to have three different types of chemo medications taken intravenously four times per week, then three, then two, down to once per week. As God began to heal through the medications my treatments were reduced to every other week.

While sitting in the hospital's designated chemo treatment rooms I began to witness to the other patients encouraging them with the Word of God. Throughout the entire process I went from a size 12 to a size 4. Good is still good. I never lost my hair. I only got sick once from the treatment and eventually regained my weight.

On January 3, 2001 the results of my follow-up exam was phenomenal. My oncologist looked at me, once, twice, three times interchangeably while looking at my labs on his computer. He took off his glasses looked at me again and asked, "How do you feel?" I replied, "I feel great!"
Based on that response and my lab results, he canceled the remaining treatments. Thank God I did not need any more chemo. I didn't hesitate to give praise glory and honor to my God for healing me right in the presence of my doctor. My entire treatment team was happy for me.

I was so excited I wanted the whole world to know what God

had done for me. That Sunday I testified to the body of Christ at my church where so many of my family and friends had supported me through all of my heartaches and struggles from the break-up with my first fiancée to the loss of my husband and my mother.

As I look back over my life and as I think things over I can truly say I've been blessed. I have a testimony of God's healing. He has healed me emotionally, physically and spiritually. I will forever stand on the word of God no matter what the situation may be.

My Song of Praise
"I love you Jesus. I worship and adore you. Just want to tell you, Lord I love you more than anything."
Lamar Campbell and Spirit of Praise

Scripture References

Proverbs 14:12 - There is a way which seemeth right unto a man, but the end thereof *are* the ways of death.

II Timothy 2:15 - Study to shew thyself approved unto God, a workman that needeth not to be ashamed, rightly dividing the word of truth.

I Corinthians 6:18 - Flee fornication. Every sin that a man doeth is without the body; but he that committeth fornication sinneth against his own body.

I Corinthians 4:5 - Therefore judge nothing before the time, until the Lord come, who both will bring to light the hidden things of darkness, and will make manifest the counsels of the hearts: and then shall every man have praise of God.

II Corinthians 5:17 - Therefore if any man *be* in Christ, *he is* a new creature: old things are passed away; behold, all things are become new.

I Samuel 1:2 - And he had two wives; the name of the one *was* Hanna, and the name of the other Peninnah: and Peninnah had children, but Hanna had no children. (7) And *as* he did so year by year, when she went up to the house of the Lord, so she provoked her; therefore she wept, and did not eat.

Hebrews 10:25 - Not forsaking the assembling of ourselves together, as the manner of some *is*; but exhorting *one another*: and so much the more, as ye see the day approaching.

Psalm 107:20 -He sent his word and healed them and delivered them from their destructions.

Psalm 30:5b – weeping may endure for a night, but joy *cometh* in the morning.

Matthew 5:44 – But I say unto you, Love your enemies, bless them that curse you, do good to them that hate you, pray for them which despitefully use you, and persecute you;

Luke 19:13 – and said unto them, Occupy till I come.

Proverbs 3:5, 6 – Trust in the Lord with all thine heart; and lean not unto thine own understanding. (6) In all thy ways acknowledge him, and he shall direct thy paths.

I Thessalonians 5:21 – Prove all things; hold fast that which is good.

Isaiah 53:1 – Who hath believed our report? and to whom is the arm of the Lord revealed?

I Thessalonians 5:18 – In everything give thanks: for this is the will of God in Christ Jesus concerning you.

II Corinthians 5:8 – We are confident, I say and willing rather to be absent from the body, and to be present with the Lord.

I Kings 19:12 – And after the earthquake a fire; *but* the LORD *was* not in the fire: and after the fire a still small voice.

Psalm 118:17 – I shall not die, but live, and declare the works of the Lord.

Personal Reflections

Chapter Six
Shelley

I met Shelley in 1993 when I became the preschool teacher for her 3 year old son. At the time she was pregnant and her pregnancy inspired me to want another baby. I am glad that I did not let her first impression be a lasting one because she appeared to be a very stern, no-nonsense woman with features resembling that of a sister from the mother land. Today she is my BFF, my sister, my Boo, Umpie (auntie) to my children and sister in-law to my husband. My daughter was born in 1994 and now our girls are sisters for life. I love you Shelley. We are truly sisters from another mother.

Shelley. I thought I was living a meaningful life filled with love, joy and peace. But that all came to a slow and painful halt. In the year of 2007 my husband of 18 years decided he wanted to be alone and in his words, take some time off to find himself. WOW!!! Okay. His plan was to go visit his parents in southern California for a week or two. Even though I felt unsettled in my spirit I agreed as if I really had control over where he went. The way he tip-toed around the house prior to leaving it seemed as if he was uncertain about his decision. May 19 (my birthday) was the day he left with his luggage in tow for his two week sabbatical.

Well...two weeks turned into four. I didn't want to be pushy so I continued to wait and pray for him. All the while I'm left at home with our two children. Our oldest son was about to graduate from high school and our daughter was going into high school along with three wonderful foster children. I was employed part-time, in school and actively involved in ministry. It seemed like a lot but by the grace of God it worked (Philippians 4:13).

When my husband returned to the city we had recently relocated to he failed to come home to me and our family. Then he dropped a bomb when he told me that he was going to be renting a room from one of his co-workers. My whole world exploded. I felt abandoned, hurt and extremely upset. Knowing him he had something else to tell me but was not man enough to do so.

Sure enough what's done in the dark comes to light. He invited me to meet him at my favorite spot... Barnes and Noble. A place I went to get away from home to relax, drink coffee and of course to read. The place I visited for pleasure suddenly became a place of sorrow and sadness when he told me that he felt we had grown apart and that he wanted to be alone. I don't remember too much after that. It seemed as if the room began to spin around and around. My legs began to tremble as my eyes filled with water. I felt sick to my stomach as I looked at him in disbelief.

He continued to express his feelings about not wanting to do the *"Christian thing."* In other words he was telling me that he did not want to be saved anymore. I began to wonder were you ever saved...Negro. After living with this man for 18 years all of a sudden he began to denounce the God of my salvation by saying, "It was too hard to be saved, too many rules. You can't do this and you can't do that." It all sounded blah, blah, blah to me. But when we met it was in the house of the Lord. He knew I was a church girl.

Now I felt like the enemy had played me. Was he a fake and a phony pretending to love God so that he could get a saved wife? All of those thoughts quickly raced through my mind while I sat quietly trying to catch my breath and soothe my breaking heart in the midst of strange people who I felt could see right through me.

I remember thinking oh my God! Did he have a calculated plan to separate me from my church family and friends in Oakland just to move us all the way to Stockton so that he could abandon us. Even after he had agreed that we could open our home to more foster children. Now he was walking out on all of us. Feeling it was time to leave I asked him about my theory. He looked at me dumbfounded. He had no answers. I wanted to attack him like a bear at a picnic. But the Holy Ghost constrained me.

The drive home started out quiet until I cried out..."*Oh God! What am I going to do now?*" I had poured my entire life into my family. Now it felt as if I was losing it all like water running down the street. Before exiting my car and I don't know how I got home that day...I screamed, shouted and beat up on the steering wheel. Then I had to pull myself together go into the house and make dinner for my children.

All of this occurred during the time my son was about to graduate from high school and move to Sacramento to attend college. Once again God blessed and I was able to purchase his senior package and get him across the stage (Philippians 4:19). As usual there was no support from his dad who did manage to attend the graduation.

I was glad about that. I did not want my son to be hurt and disappointed during this monumental time in his life. At that time our children did not know their dad was no longer in the home mainly because he was never really that active in their lives.

As time went on my life became a living nightmare. My ex-husband had so many secrets. He sold the family car in turn for a convertible (single man's car). The children and I were not excited. I had been a stay at home wife and mother. He managed the finances and never explained anything to me. I felt like there was someone else in the picture and when I asked him he did not deny that he had met another woman.

One day he had the nerve to bring her by the house in his new car. At the time I was holding a water hose in my hand and my first thought was to flood the car. I positioned myself from in front of her and asked him who she was. He replied you don't know her and yes I am in love with her and yes we are sleeping together...looking at me as if I should have known.

Speechless and breathless I managed to walk my broken hearted self- down the street. Hoping that he would take this opportunity to drive away and he did. God, hallelujah... kept me calm (Isaiah 26:3).

As if all that was not enough my hours from work got cut. The owner of the house I was renting had not been paying her mortgage and it was foreclosed on. I had three months to move. Once again the favor of God was shown when I met a property owner while I was house hunting. He had just purchased four houses and when I told him my situation he let me move into one of them and all I had to pay was the first month's rent (Numbers 6:24, 25). Thank you, Jesus.

One day Mr. T called me. In one breathe he apologized for leaving his family and in the next breathe he asked if he could come and stay with us for at least two weeks until his new residence got ready. This would have been the perfect time for me to execute some vengeance but the God in me would not let me say no (Romans 12:19, 21).

He stayed downstairs in the room I used for my prayer closet for ten days. The Spirit of God in that place would not let him be comfortable. He got sick, had diarrhea and even tried to get drunk. Seeing that he was moving out a second time I asked him what he was planning to do. I could not allow him to keep running in and out of our lives. Sounds like the Gap Band, *"you can't keep runnin in an outta my life."* I know.

He replied that he would file for divorce. It was hard to not let him see the hurt and pain I was experiencing at that very moment. It took all of the Holy Ghost in me to say, "file the papers and I will sign them." He said, "We are living two separate lives and I want to move on."

Have you ever experienced a time in your life when it seemed like prayer and fasting did not work? Well this was that time for me. I fasted and prayed for two weeks but my breakthrough was only temporary. Depression covered my house (which no longer felt like a home) from upstairs to downstairs. It crept into every bedroom, the living room, the kitchen, everywhere there was an open space. I felt heavy and empty at the same time. There were days when I struggled just to get out of my dark lonely bed in my dark and gloomy room (Isaiah 61:3).

My daughter suffered as well. She felt abandoned and rejected by her dad. Because of my own depression I didn't have what she needed to help deal with her emotions. Her school life suffered to the point of where two of her teachers called with concern about her lack of interest in academics. When I told them our story they broke down and cried. They cared so much for my daughter and I know that God touched their hearts and gave them the desire to want to assist us.

When I received notice that the divorce papers had been filed that's when it hit me. This was really happening. It was not a dream. My marriage was really over. It seemed like my life was over. It is so true that going through a divorce is like losing a loved one to death. In spite of all that the bills kept coming. I finally petitioned God to touch the man I once called my husband so that he would pay child support (I John 5:14 -15).

He began paying but he did so inconsistently. I continued to trust God to supply our needs as I continued to pay my tithes. We got another breakthrough when the court ordered alimony began to come in. Thank you, Jesus (I Thessalonians 5:18).

Just when I thought the smoke was starting to clear I got a phone call from my mother's doctor. He informed me that she was extremely ill and in need of emergency surgery. You would think that my other siblings would have stepped up to the plate knowing that I was going through in my own life, but that was not the case. I had to rearrange my life to go to Texas. This meant that my foster children would have to go to respite (foster care babysitting) and my daughter would have to stay with her dad even though she didn't want to. That was her only option.

Eventually my mom's health deteriorated to the point of needing a leg amputation. I packed up my belongings, put them into storage and moved to Texas. The owner agreed to hold my house for two months. Who does that? While I was in Texas attending to my mom's affairs I got a call from my neighbor who informed me that someone was moving into my house and that they only came at night (John10:10).

I called the owner and asked if he knew what was going on and of course he did not. After further investigation it was discovered that someone had been squatting in the house. Now I don't have anywhere to come home to. The owner assured me that he would look into this situation and help me find another place to live.

Once my mom's health stabilized I returned to Stockton.

I was homeless and had no job. My daughter and I had to live with her best friend's mom so that she could continue to go to school. A payment I had made for my truck while in Texas was stolen which made matters worse when it was repossessed from my son in Sacramento. I'm a witness to the saying when it rains it pours (Isaiah 59:19).

For days I felt tired, worn and utterly beat down as depression set in again. I isolated myself from people, places and things. I had no support from the church I had served in so faithfully. My siblings seemed to think that I had it all together and didn't need them. I thank God for my Bay Area friends who kept me in prayer even though they didn't know everything I was going through. I grieved alone.

I eventually started to visit different churches. One day God in His faithfulness was there to see about me in one of those services. He knew I was depleted as I felt his Spirit breathe life into me. All I could do was praise Him. Like Karen Clark-Sheard's song, *"if I can't say a word I'll just wave my hands."* That's all I could do. The Holy Ghost interceded for me (Romans 8:26). My worship changed that day as I felt the power of God refresh, renew, refill and lift me.

My praise and worship was restored and blessing God again opened doors for me. Everything the devil stole from me was restored including my truck (Isaiah 61:7). Through my former landlord who felt indebted to me I moved into a new house. I found a new job and the alimony became court ordered. I can sleep at night without having to take sleep aids (Proverbs 3:24). Now that our divorce is final healing is taking place for me and my children who are now living out their young adult lives (Jeremiah 17:14).

"Heal me, O Lord, and I shall be healed; save me, and I shall be saved: for thou art my praise."
Jeremiah 17:14

Without God I never would have made it through brokenness, loneliness, depression and loss of material things as a result of my divorce. I now feel empowered to encourage other women on this journey to my destiny. By taking life one day at a time as I continue to trust in the true and living God to always provide for me spiritually, physically and emotionally.

In loving memory of my mom Ophelia Gooden

My Song of Praise
"Jesus is the best thing that ever happened to me."
Reverend James Cleveland

Scripture References

Philippians 4:13 - I can do all things through Christ which strengtheneth me.

Philippians 4:19 - But my God shall supply all your need according to his riches in glory by Christ Jesus.

Isaiah 26:3 - Thou wilt keep *him* in perfect peace, *whose* mind *is* stayed *on thee:* because he trusteth in thee.

Numbers 6:24, 25 - The Lord bless thee and keep thee: (25) The Lord make his face shine upon thee, and be gracious unto thee:

Romans 12:19b - for it is written, Vengeance is mine; I will repay, saith the Lord.

Romans 12:21 - Be not overcome of evil, but overcome evil with good.

Isaiah 61:3 - To appoint unto them that mourn in Zion, to give unto them beauty for ashes, the oil of joy for mourning, the garment of praise for the spirit of heaviness;

I John 5:14, 15 - and this is the confidence that we have in him, that if we ask any thing according to his will, he heareth us: (15) And if we know that he hear us, whatsoever we ask, we know that we have the petitions that we desired of him.

I Thessalonians 5:18 - In everything give thanks: for this is the will of God in Christ Jesus concerning you.

John 10:10 - The thief cometh not, but for to steal, and to

kill, and to destroy: I am come that they might have life, and that they might have it more abundantly.

Isaiah 59:19b - When the enemy shall come in like a flood, the Spirit of the Lord shall lift up a standard against him.

Romans 8:26 - Likewise the Spirit also helpeth our infirmities: for we know not what we should pray for as we ought: but the Spirit itself maketh intercession for us with groaning s which cannot be uttered.

Isaiah 61:7 - For your shame *ye shall have* double:

Proverbs 3:24 - When thou liest down, thou shalt not be afraid: yea, thou shalt lie down, and thy sleep shall be sweet.

Jeremiah 17:14 - Heal me, O Lord, and I shall be healed; save me, and I shall be saved: for thou art my praise.

Personal Reflections

Chapter Seven
Loretta

I met Loretta in 2007. She approached me about being a part of the staff I was putting together for a women's support group at the church we attended together. She had an uninhibited smile and laughter that filled the room when it was expressed. Loretta willingly and openly shared her testimony in one of our first sessions. Since then we have shared many personal life experiences over lunch, dinner or at some kind of community festival. It is really great when you can spend time getting to know a sister away from church. I love you Loretta.

Loretta. When I was eight years old my father abandoned my mother while she was pregnant with their eleventh child. I was the fifth child and the second oldest girl. My sister was nine years older than I was so when she turned 18 she got married and moved out.

My mom was constantly depressed and unhappy. At nine years old I felt responsible for my other siblings. I would get them and me ready for school. I prepared our breakfasts and lunches. When school was out I would cook dinner and clean house. I literally became their mother.

My mom was drunk and lonely most of the time. She allowed different men to come in and out of the house. One day her live in boyfriend took advantage of me. I was only nine years old when he took me to the basement and raped me. He was an abusive man who beat my mom all the time. So I believed him when he threatened to hurt me if I told anyone. Because we didn't talk about sex or sexual abuse in those days I felt there was no one to tell.

After my innocence had been taken away my life was never the same. I became withdrawn, my smile was gone and I hated my mother. I hated my dad even more because he was no longer there to protect me. My grandmother was the one who took us to church. If it had not been for her we would not have had any church upbringing. I even hated my grandmother because she kept telling me about Jesus who was supposed to love me (John 3:16). I couldn't understand that kind of love. If he loved me why did I have to be a mother to my siblings, carry the guilt and shame of being raped and not be able to tell anyone but this God who I didn't believe exists (Hebrews 11:6).

At the age of twelve I began hanging out with older kids because I felt I was mature and more physically developed than my peers. So whatever they did I did. If they smoked weed I did too. If they drank alcohol I did too. Although I really didn't like it...I realized that it helped me forget all of the hurt and pain I was feeling inside. However, hanging with older kids only made me a target for more abuse. I became the victim of rape again. Because of that I needed to do something stronger than weed and alcohol. I took uppers. I took downers. I took acid. I took anything I could get my hands on to help me forget.

I hated myself. I wanted to die. I started to plan how I could end my life. Just when I thought I had a plan to end my life my grandmother took us to church. The devil said no but God said yes (Psalm 118:17). That Sunday the preacher spoke on how committing suicide was the ultimate sin because you cannot ask God for forgiveness.

Now I couldn't even kill myself as planned. I couldn't see myself living in hell on earth then dying and living in hell eternally. Well then I thought ...I'll just put myself into situations where someone else would have to kill me. I got myself into a situation that I thought would assist my suicide. Again this God intervened (Psalm 46:1). When I came home from school one day my mom had packed up everything and we were moving from west Oakland to east Oakland. There was no mention of moving that morning when I left to go to school.

Even though we now lived in east Oakland I would still catch the bus to the old neighborhood to hang out. One night while I was waiting for the bus I accepted a ride from this man who took me to Berkeley instead of west Oakland. I was gang raped by a number of guys. I really thought I would die that night. I wanted to die. Another man showed up and took me to his apartment four blocks from where I lived. I was totally hysterical. He felt sorry for me and took me home.

I began to question this Jesus my grandmother told me about. I wanted to know why I was born. Why I had to continue to go through so much pain. What did I do to deserve so much pain? I hated myself even more. At 16 I graduated (not from school) to even harder drugs. I began snorting cocaine. I came to the realization that this was my lot in life and that nothing good was ever going to become of me. I had been raped so many times in my short life. I thought that was how it went. Men took what they wanted and I had no say so about it.

I didn't know I had a choice until I was hanging out with some girls and they were talking about when they lost their virginity. I was shocked and of course I couldn't say anything because my experiences were so different.

I got married when I was 20 years old to an abusive man. He introduced me to free basing. We smoked dope and fought. He had a lot of other women. He treated me like dirt and I felt like I deserved it. Things got so bad I wanted to kill him. I even bought a gun but I called my younger brother to come rescue me and my child from him before I actually went that far (I Corinthians 10:13). Yes...by now I had a daughter. My marriage lasted two years but I stayed married to him for ten years in order to not make that mistake again.

I was searching for love (I John 4:8). I had an empty whole in my heart and I just wanted it filled. I thought I could fill it with substances. I started smoking crack cocaine and I got married again to someone else...who as time went on helped me to turn my life around. Together we had two sons. I didn't know how to love my children because I didn't know how to love myself. By then I was in my thirties. I was good and tired, sick and tired of my life being like it was.

One night after getting high, I proclaimed "I'm tired." I demanded, "God if you are really real then show yourself to me" (Acts 2:21). When I cried out God came in and began delivering me from all of my addictions. I know it was him because in and of myself I could not stop abusing drugs on my own. It took someone great and powerful to deliver me (Joel 2:32).

> *"And it shall come to pass, that whosoever shall call on the name of the Lord shall be delivered:"*
> **Joel 2:32**

The desire for alcohol was gone. The desire for drugs was gone. God began to do a new thing in my life and the life of my husband as well (Isaiah 43:19). He changed me from the inside out. I now have my smile back and I am free from all guilt and shame.

Since my husband had a stronger church background than I did he got us into a bible teaching church where we learned the word of God and how to live victoriously (Acts 26:22). I can happily say that I now live a saved, Holy Ghost filled life as a born again believer (John 3:7).

We were able to raise our children in church. They were too young to remember the kind of life we lived before Jesus Christ transformed us. We were blessed to love them with the love of God. I now am able to love my children and others unconditionally because God showed me how to love myself for the first time in my life.

My Song of Praise
"To God be the glory for all the things...He has done."
Andrae Crouch

Scripture References

John 3:16 – For God so loved the world, that he gave his only begotten Son, that whosoever believeth in him should not perish, but have everlasting life.

Hebrews 11:6 – But without faith *it is* impossible to please *him*: for he that cometh to God must believe that he is, and *that* he is a rewarder of them that diligently seek him.

Psalm 118:17 – I shall not die, but live, and declare the works of the Lord.

Psalm 46:1 – God is our refuge and strength, a very present help in trouble.

I Corinthians 10:13 – There hath no temptation taken you but such as is common to man: but God *is* faithful, who will not suffer you to be tempted above that ye are able; but will with the temptation also make a way to escape, that ye may be able to bear *it*.

I John 4:8 – He that loveth not knoweth not God; for God is love.

Acts 2:21– And it shall come to pass, *that* whosoever shall call on the name of the Lord shall be saved.

Joel 2:32 – And it shall come to pass, *that* whosoever shall call on the name of the Lord shall be delivered:

Isaiah 43:19 - Behold, I will do a new thing; now it shall spring forth; shall ye not know? I will even make a way in the wilderness, *and* rivers in the desert.

Acts 26:22 - Having therefore obtained help of God, I continue unto this day, witnessing both to small and great,

John 3:7 - Marvel not that I said unto thee, Ye must be born again.

Personal Reflections

Chapter Eight
Ashli

When I met Ashli in 2009 it was with her husband Ken and their 9 month old daughter Ashlyn. As time went on I realized that she and I had similar personalities. We both possess a strong calmness. We are resilient, diligent and always living in the here and now while planning for the future.

I was honored when she entrusted me to be the childcare provider for her children. Ever since that first encounter we have been a part of each other's lives. I had the pleasure of attending her daughter's 6th birthday celebration in her kindergarten classroom. That's when I realized that as long as I lived I would be there for every monumental event in their lives. Thank you Ashli for my two beautiful nieces even though they still call me "teacher." I love you Ashli and your beautiful daughters.

Ashli. In 1999 I met Ken in our high school chemistry class. I was a senior and he was a junior. We joked and flirted with each other right away (chemistry) and quickly became friends. Our friendship led to us becoming a couple...soon to be known as high school sweethearts. Life and love was good as we knew it.

Ken and I attended college for a few years in California before he was offered and accepted a football scholarship to a University in Missouri. Once he relocated to Missouri I had the opportunity to visit him on two occasions during his first semester. He came home that summer and proposed to me. We had dated for five years... so of course I said yes (Proverbs 18:22).

Within two months we were marching down the aisle in a beautiful ceremony before God our families and friends (Genesis 2:24). This was a wonderful time in my life. I had married my best friend. We moved to Missouri and I also enrolled in school. We were happy and in love. That love created our first daughter, Ashlyn two years after our marriage. All my life I had wanted a daughter and she was truly a blessing from God. I loved being a mother and Ken adored our daughter.

Ken had difficulty finding a job to his liking after he graduated from college, so he began to look for employment in California. However I still had a year left before my education was complete. That is when I realized how selfish Ken was. He moved to California three months before Ashlyn and I were able to join him, because I was in the middle of a semester. I wanted to stay in Missouri and finish school, but Ken had already made the decision for the both of us. So we relocated back to California.

When I returned to California I was happy to be reunited with my family, friends and my husband who had found a job (II Thessalonians 3:10). However my emotions were mixed. I was happy while at the same time somewhat unhappy because I was not able to finish school which is what I had wanted to accomplish when I moved to Missouri. I felt moving back to California was a sacrifice I had to make for our family but that sacrifice was not appreciated.

Two years later I got pregnant with our second daughter Alexis. My happiness soon began to diminish while my husband was walking on cloud nine. Determined to complete my college education I returned to school. Ken and I were arguing a lot because he was working in excess and not spending enough time with us. He argued that he was working to provide for his family but to me providing for your family also included social and emotional support with your availability and presence. I didn't get married to be a single parent.

Six months into my pregnancy my suspensions that Ken was cheating on me were coming to light (I Corinthians 4:5). He was staying out late and sometimes not even coming home. While he was in the shower one morning I went through his phone and confirmed my suspensions. They say a woman on a mission does a better job at investigating than the FBI. This is true.

I conducted my own investigation and found out everything I needed to know about this other woman, but the most troubling discovery is that she was his boss. Not only was she his boss but they both worked in the administration offices of the very school I attended. I was heartbroken (Psalm 34:18).

The stress and heartache of my husband cheating on me caused me to go into labor prematurely. My newborn came into the world six weeks early and had to stay in the NICU (neonatal intensive care unit) for 19 days. This was horrible for me because I was alone with her every day while still caring for Ashlyn.

After Alexis came home Ken continued having a relationship with this woman...his boss. He did not try to conceal his intentions so my only recourse was to put him out. Although my heart was broken I allowed him to come back several times throughout that year because I wanted so bad to have my family intact. We were married and I felt I needed to do all I could to save our marriage (Matthew 19:6). But there were too many discrepancies in his behavior and I just could not deal with his lies. My two daughters were depending on me to care for them, so I had to finally let go and let God.

Not only did he abandon me but...Baby Alexis did not know who he was when he did come around. He never got up in the middle of the night to feed her or rock her to sleep. I can count the number of times on one hand that he changed her diapers or cared for her when she was sick. Due to Alexis' preemi status she suffered from minor respiratory problems that required her to visit the doctor weekly. Again Ken was not around for those visits. He didn't seem to care that Alexis would cry when he tried to hold her. You would think that a father would be concerned about not having a relationship with his baby. Again I could clearly see how selfish he was.

Ashlyn was also abandoned by her father. She was very close to him. He would call and talk to her but really...a phone conversation with a two year old... not very fruitful. Trying to get child support from Ken was a b-a-t-t-l-e. After a lengthy court process he finally began to pay.

By the time monies started to come in a lot of financial damages had already been done. In attempts to support myself I began taking out loans just to keep food on the table, keep the PG&E on, gas in the car so I could drop the girls off at daycare go to work and then back home again. Thank God for a childcare provider who knew my situation had compassion on me and my girls and cared for them as if I was still paying for them to attend.

We finally filed for a divorce two years after being separated. We were not married long enough to fulfill the American dream of purchasing a home together. I never got my two car garage or my white picket fence with a dog inside the yard. The dynamics of divorce continues to be a lengthy process due to disagreements between the two of us. Hopefully I can officially close this chapter soon.

Ken now lives with his girlfriend in a relationship that was formed as a result of his infidelity to me. Since I want my daughters to have a relationship with their father I allow them to be around her. To me...correct me if I'm wrong but a woman who would knowingly take part in breaking up a marriage is not the type of person a mother would want around her daughters. It is clearly understood that she is not to take part in mothering my daughters. Ken and I are on the same page about that. The girls have a great time when they are with their father and I am comfortable in knowing that.

I am in awe of how God brought me through this entire ordeal and I didn't totally lose my mind (Psalm 73:26). The devil would have me think that I made a mistake by living according to what I believed was God's order for love and marriage before children. Trying to be a supportive wife I know that I did everything right. I used to think...what if I had been more attractive or sexier. I have beat myself up with "what ifs" numerous times over the years. But the devil is a liar. I know that I was created just the way God wanted me to be (Psalm 139:14). My girls are definitely a gift from God. They have given me purpose and I know that they are a part of my destiny.

> ### *"I will praise thee; for I am fearfully and wonderfully made:"*
> ### Psalm 139:14

When we exchanged our vows in the presence of God with our families and friends as witnesses I believed it would be forever. Ken was the one who broke our marital vows along with my heart and jeopardized the health and safety of me and our daughters. I no longer make excuses or blame myself for his mistakes. Thank you, Jesus.

The bible says in Romans 8:28 that all things work together for them who love the Lord and have been called according to His purpose. I know that to be true now but I couldn't see it when I was going through this nightmare with Ken.

I have since received my BS in Human Services and I'm currently pursuing my Master's Degree in Social Work through an on-line program at the University of Southern California (USC). I stayed in church with my girls even though there were days when I didn't want to face the world and felt like my life was over(Lamentation 3:21-23). I know without a shadow of doubt that my faith in the true and living God caused me to be victorious in this situation (Romans 8:37).

I wish I could say that I have totally forgiven Ken but I can't say that I have. Forgiveness is a process and I am praying and trusting God to help me get to that point. I also know that I will remarry one day because just like God made Adam from the dust of the earth I believe He can also make someone who will love me and my daughters (Psalm 37:4).

My Song of Praise
"Never would have made it without you."
Pastor Marvin Sapp

Scripture References

Proverbs 18:22 – *Whoso* findeth a wife findeth a good *thing,* and obtaineth favor of the Lord.

Genesis 2:24 – Therefore shall a man leave his father and his mother, and shall cleave unto his wife: and they shall be one flesh.

II Thessalonians 3:10 – For even when we were with you, this we commanded you, that if any would not work, neither should he eat.

Psalm 34:18 – The Lord is nigh unto them that are of a broken heart; and saveth such as be of a contrite spirit.

I Corinthians 4:5 – Therefore judge nothing before the time, until the Lord come, who both will bring to light the hidden things of darkness, and will make manifest the counsels of the hearts:

Matthew 19:6 – Wherefore they are no more twain, but one flesh. What therefore God hath joined together, let not man put asunder.

Psalm 73:26 – My flesh and my heart faileth: *but* God *is* the strength of my heart, and my portion forever.

Psalm 139:14 – I will praise thee; for I am fearfully *and* wonderfully made: marvelous are thy works: and *that* my soul knoweth right well.

Lamentation 3:21-23 – This I recall to my mind, therefore have I hope. (22) *It is of* the Lord's mercies that we are not consumed, because his compassions fail not. (23) *They are* new every morning: great *is* thy faithfulness.

Romans 8:37 – Nay, in all these things we are more than conquerors through him that loved us.

Psalm 37:4 - Delight thyself also in the Lord; and he shall give thee the desires of thine heart.

Personal Reflections

Chapter Nine
Meredith

For years I had watched Meredith from across the sanctuary at the church we now attend together. She moves with poise and confidence. Her praise and worship to God is sincere and uninhibited. I had only acknowledged her presence with a wave and a smile not sure of how I would be received if I tried to do more. One day in the fellowship hall of our church the Lord orchestrated a divine encounter. OMG! She was warm, articulate and open. I was amazed at her candidness. We talked like we were old girlfriends. Thank you, Meredith for being transparent from the very beginning. I love you.

Meredith. My parents divorced when I was 3 years old. I don't remember my father being in the home. Following the divorce of my parents, we moved to San Francisco but my siblings and I would spend summers with my paternal grandparents in Sacramento. I loved that time. My aunts, uncles and cousins all lived in the same area. We would play outside every day.

Then every Saturday afternoon, Grandma would press our hair for church on Sunday. Which consisted of all day church, 9 am Sunday school, 10:30 church service; out at 2:30, home for a Sunday dinner of fried chicken, mashed potatoes, corn, and homemade sweet potato pie, peach cobbler or lemon pound cake, then back for 6:00 pm service.

We attended YPWW (Young People Willing Workers) Thursday evenings, Vacation Bible School and every other church activity that included children. Every summer from the time

I was 3 until I turned 13. I was raised in the church – raised COGIC (Church of God in Christ) (II Timothy 3:15). But then we stopped going to Sacramento and I stopped going to church.

I was 14 when I was molested by a girlfriend's father. At the time, I did not realize it was called molestation. I just remember going over to my friend's house after school one day. Hugging and kissing her mother first, then her father. But this time he reached up and grabbed my left breast all while sticking his tongue in my mouth. I pulled back. I looked around to see if my friend or her mother noticed and no one seemed to notice. From that day on, I never hugged or kissed him again. I also never told anyone and I don't know why. Not sure if I didn't want to cause any trouble for my family or my friend's family. I grew up, moved on and stayed outside of the church.

I married when I was 21. I was determined to stay married and break what I considered the "family curse of divorce". Both of my grandparents divorced; my favorite aunt and uncle divorced. Another uncle and aunt divorced. My best friend's parents were divorced. I wanted to break the "generational curse", give my children a home with two parents.

When I came home 3 days after delivering our first child, someone who I thought was a good friend, felt it was her duty to tell me my husband had another woman in our house while I was in the hospital – WOW!!! Although I was devastated, I wanted to "break the curse".

After my husband had an affair a couple years later, I received a living room full of new furniture – devastated again. After another affair a year later, I received a full length mink coat and a mink jacket – heartbroken again (Psalm 34:18). We had our second child a few years later.

He had another affair sometime after that - I got a new Mercedes. I still wanted to break the curse. My husband had many more affairs throughout our marriage.

Sometimes I wondered, "What kind of woman I was who would stay in a relationship that brought me such heartache, feelings of intimacy inadequacy and loss of trust in both men and women (II Corinthians 13:5). Why was breaking the "curse" so important?

Then one morning, I woke up tired. And to this day, I'm not sure what had changed in me because nothing special happened the night before, no argument...nothing special. I told him I was tired and that I was leaving. He cried, begged, called his dad to come talk to me (I loved my father-in-law and we had a wonderful father/daughter relationship).

As I was packing, my father-in-law came over trying to explain his son's actions. He told me that "I had been put on a high pedestal, and those other women really meant nothing to him. That I was his true love" - WOW! My children and I left that same day and moved in with my mom and step-dad.

Eight months after the move, I was spending the night at my sister's home in Richmond. I had just bought a new car from a friend of theirs that worked at a dealership. The following morning, I was heading to the grocery store for a pack of cigarettes when I noticed a car following me. I didn't recognize the car at first. When I pulled into the parking lot of the store, the car came along side me. It was my husband, in his girlfriend's car, and he began shooting at me. He began shooting at me. I couldn't believe it.

As I ducked and sped away, he continued following and shooting at me until I got back to my sister's home. I left my

80 brand new car in the middle of the street and ran into her house. Fortunately I was not hit – not all blessings are financial (Psalm 91:11).

I called the police and was later told he was arrested when he pulled into our home in Pacifica (Isaiah 54:17). Through his lawyer, I was told he wasn't trying to hurt me.
He just wanted to scare me into coming home and dropping the divorce proceedings. The police department dropped the charges without consulting with me. I contacted them demanding the charges be reinstated. They thought that I would not follow-through with the charges, because most women don't and they assumed I was like "most women".

He was convicted of discharging a firearm in a public place. His actions enabled the judge to award me primary custody of our children and force him to sign the divorce papers – not all blessings are financial.

After the divorce, I began receiving collection calls for charges my ex-husband had accumulated over the 2 years it took before the divorce was final. Because I was still legally married at the time, and working, (he was not working at the time) I was being asked to pay over $50,000 in debt. I had to file for bankruptcy. WOW!

My children's father did not pay child support while they were growing up. But I did not stop him from seeing them nor did I speak negatively of him to them. As a product of divorce, I always felt I missed out on "something" not having a two parent household and I did not want them to "miss out". My children had the opportunity to develop their own impression of their father. And their relationship with him today, is indicative of his actions while they were growing up. He still owes me $20,000 in arrears for child support. The past is just that. I can't change it (Philippians 3:13).

> *"But this one thing I do, forgetting those things which are behind. And reaching forth unto those things which are before,"*
> **Philippians 3:13**

I have 2 beautiful children out of a not-so-pretty marriage - blessings (Romans 8:28). I worked 2 jobs, went to school and was a single parent. There were times when I didn't know how I was going to provide for my girls. But every time we were down to pennies, God provided (Psalm 27:13). Sometimes it came down to the tips I would receive driving tour buses. After I got off work, I could use my tip money to get groceries to last until payday.

During this time with my girls, I began having an inner feeling that I was not going to live beyond the age of 42. I can't explain the feeling, but I knew it was real. It wasn't a daily concern, but every now and then the feeling would hang over me. So I began preparing. Taking out life insurance and putting things in order. I never told anyone about this feeling and I still did not have a church home.

It was in November the month of my 41st year of life. I owned a business with a mentor of mine. One day, her cousin asked us to do some work for her. We met and I found out she was the Pastor of a church in Oakland. I began going to church again and the day after my 42nd birthday, I died to my old self and I was born again (John 3:6, 7). Look at God!

My current husband and I have been together for 25 years. My children are college graduates and independent women. They have a praying mother who knows one day they too will come to accept the Lord as their personal Savior. I thank God I knew enough to baptize them as children and to occasionally take them to church. Whenever they have children, they'll have a praying grandmother.

I was born again 14 years ago. I am so grateful God loved me during the times I didn't love myself (I John 4:19). I am so grateful I had a praying Grandmother and Auntie. I am so grateful I was raised in the church.

I am a strong woman. I am glad I don't look like what I've been through. I hold my head up high because He created me to be somebody. Not necessarily famous or well known by the world's standards, but He has a plan for me. He knew all of the mistakes I would make but He still chose me (Matthew 22:14). I'm working hard to be what He's called me to be.

My Song of Praise
"I'm still here and it's by the grace of God."
Dorinda Clark-Cole

Scripture References

II Timothy 3:15-And that from a child thou hast known the holy scriptures, which are able to make thee wise unto salvation through faith which is in Christ Jesus.

Psalm 34:18 – The Lord *is* nigh unto them that are of a broken heart; and saveth such as be of a contrite spirit.

II Corinthians 13:5 - Examine yourselves, whether ye be in the faith; prove your own selves. Know ye not your own selves, how that Jesus Christ is in you, except ye be reprobates?

Psalm 91:11 – For he shall give his angels charge over thee, to keep thee in all thy ways.

Isaiah 54:17 – No weapon that is formed against thee shall prosper; and every tongue *that* shall rise against thee in judgment thou shalt condemn. This *is* the heritage of the servants of the Lord, and their righteousness *is* of me, saith the Lord.

Philippians 3:13 – Brethren, I count not myself to have apprehended: but *this* one thing *I do,* forgetting those things which are behind, and reaching forth unto those things which are before,

Romans 8:28 – And we know that all things work together for good to them that love God, to them who are the called according to *his* purpose.

Psalm 27:13 – I had fainted, unless I had believed to see the goodness of the Lord in the land of the living.

John 3: 6, 7 – That which is born of the flesh is flesh; and that which is born of the Spirit is spirit. (7) Marvel not that I said unto thee, Ye must be born again.

I John 4:19 – We love him, because he first loved us.

Matthew 22:14 – For many are called, but few are *chosen.*

Personal Reflections

Chapter Ten
Holly

I introduced myself to Holly one night in 2012 at the Nor Cal (Northern California) Holy Convocation. I had previously heard Holly share a portion of her testimony during a Tuesday night bible study at the church we attended together. I was intrigued by Holly because on Sunday mornings I would always see her leave out of the sanctuary as soon as the benediction was given which did not allow anyone the opportunity to interact with her. So that night when we sat beside each other in church that was my opportunity to get acquainted with her. I asked Holly if she would be willing to share her story for this project and she was.

Thank God for the blood of Jesus that washes and cleanses us because after she had shared with me all that the Lord had brought her through I felt like I needed to take a shower. Since then I have grown to appreciate the many facets of her personality and the woman of God she has truly become. I love you Holly.

Holly. Here I was. I had just finished receiving my Master's degree from one of the most prestigious universities in the world and I wanted to die. I was lonely confused and angry. Why did it seem as though my life had gone wrong. I had followed the rules. I had crossed my T's and dotted my I's but even educated I felt like a misfit. My feeling like a misfit had begun years earlier and no matter what the external accomplishments signified, the internal damage had been done.

God spoke to me and said there was work to be done,

internal work. Work that when it was complete would leave me equipped to carry out His purpose. I'd gone as far as I could go without addressing the psychological issues I had developed as a child such as Post Traumatic Stress Disorder (PTSD), Major Depression and Dissociative Identity Disorder as a result of long term, repeated sexual molestation.

God told me that if I didn't fix what was wrong with me internally, no matter the external acquisition, the emptiness would never go away and I would never heal. After receiving God's instruction I began my journey of healing (Jeremiah 30:17) and by the power of God and the guidance of the Holy Spirit I am the woman I am today.

> *"I will restore you to health*
> *and heal your wounds,*
> *declares the Lord."*
> **Jeremiah 30:17**

I was born on 81st avenue in Oakland, California. When I was 4 years old my family, which consisted of my mom, my brother, two sisters and my uncle Bill moved to Sobrante Park, a subdivision of East Oakland. Ever since I can remember, I loved God and I especially enjoyed church. I was always the one who would scout the neighborhood for the church, attend and then go get my mom who would then bring the rest of the family to join (Isaiah 11:6).

I was raised in a very religious household. My mother was saved, sanctified and filled with the Holy Spirit. She didn't smoke, drink, curse, dance, play cards, go to parties or wear pants. We didn't discuss anything that wasn't holy.

I longed for my mother's affection, we all did but she was preoccupied with trying to redeem herself in the eyes of her parents. They had deemed her a tramp because her first child was born out of wedlock. I was her fifth illegitimate child and all five of us had different fathers. By the time I came along my mother just wanted somebody to save her from being the family castaway.

If someone would just marry her she could be redeemed in the eyes of my grandfather, Pastor Travis Deshields West; the Sunday School Superintendent and my grandmother Cecelia Mayola West; the Northern Conference Chairwoman of the National Baptist Church Convention and my aunt Maudess West. These three had branded my mother with a mark that only marriage could erase, hence my mother's preoccupation.

In her desperation for redemption she married schizophrenic, and in the eyes of her family, marrying wrong was worse than being a tramp. My stepfather, Herbert Hoover Benjamin Long was absolutely nuts and in addition to his psychosis was addicted to alcohol, heroin and a plethora of other substances. After he and my mother divorced he moved to Louisiana where he killed himself and the woman he married after my mother.

On the day the molestation began, I know now that my mother had every intention of paying attention to me but we had a wall phone in the kitchen and I believe it rang, causing my mother to look away which allowed me to become a rape victim. From that day on, I don't remember playing like other children. I just remember sex.

By the time I was five years old I was obese. Food had become my solace and I became a constant target for bullying and torment at school, in my neighborhood and in my home. I wanted the kids to stop teasing me. I wanted my brothers and sisters to stop calling me black and nappy headed. I wanted to belong. But I didn't, they wouldn't let me. In a desperate attempt to stop the torment I would offer sex to other children. That's all I knew.

I wanted peace. I wanted to be left alone. Most of all I wanted everybody to stop touching me. The boys told me in addition to telling all the other girls what I was and what I did, so the girls wouldn't play with me. I was alone and the only human contact I received was that of a sexual nature. I was the girl taken behind the building, and when my services were no longer required I was left behind the building until the next time. I stayed behind that building until I was 40 years old.

I met my father for the first time when I was four years old. I spent the night at his house. I remember we had pimento loaf sandwiches for dinner. The next morning he showered, got dressed and dropped me off at my mother's house. Although my father didn't molest me, he dropped me off when he was done with me and I felt thrown away. I hurt inside but what five year old knows how to communicate that type of emotional pain... pain that confirmed you're not wanted, pain that dictated your every movement, pain that confirmed what you would be when you grew up.

At 9 years old I smoked my first cigarette, at 10, I drank my first beer, at 11, I smoked my first joint, and by 12, I was on cocaine and heroin. Every substance I abused made me feel good and also made it possible for me to live in my skin. I needed something. I no longer trusted or believed in God. How could I? Where had He been through all the rapes, abuse and the pain I had experienced. Surely He was big enough to have stopped it all from happening. Maybe I wasn't worth it to Him...I guessed not.

My mom attempted to reconnect with my father but he wasn't particularly interested in her, she was a church lady. My father liked fast women, and even with 5 children out of wedlock my mother was a good girl looking for love but had gotten babies instead.

My father appeared on the scene but his motives were selfish. My father loved to eat, my mother was an excellent cook and the meals were free. My mother would tell him that I had gotten in trouble at school and that he needed to come by and discipline me. She would spend all day preparing an elaborate meal, my father would arrive, beat me and they would sit down have dinner and talk while I lay bleeding on the floor.

One night, while my mother waited for my father to arrive to beat me, I jumped out of the bathroom window and ran away, I was 12. I lived on the streets of San Francisco and I did everything I had to do, not to return home. I sold my body sometimes to eat or sometimes for a place to stay or sometimes just for a hot cup of coffee.

During the next 5 years, I was raped, robbed, shot, stabbed, thrown down a flight of stairs and set on fire. It sounds extreme and it was... but it was better than being betrayed by my mother and being beaten like a slave by my father (Psalm 27:10). My mother found me when I was 16 and after an extensive stay with San Francisco's juvenile authority's I returned home. I was seventeen.

I managed to return to school and I made up the credits needed to graduate with my class. I had turned 18 that February, graduated from high school that June and decided that I would no longer be attending church; a mandatory tradition in my home until you turned 18.

Crack cocaine hit the scene in 1981 and it became the answer to all of my problems. For the next eleven years crack was my god and I sold my soul. I've been some places and with some people and done some things for the sake of getting high that the mere thought of causes me to cringe.

I lied, cheated, stole and manipulated everything and everybody that got in my path. I've been in every jail in Northern California. I returned to prostitution with a vengeance, not for food this time but to satisfy an insatiable need to escape the pain of being me.

Once again I opened myself up to rape and abuse. I was sodomized and beaten viciously, gang raped at gun and knifepoint. I never tried to get help, I didn't want help. Who was going to help me, surely not God! I remember looking up to heaven one day and asking God, "is this all you wrote down for me?" He didn't answer so I kept using.

I used crack daily from the age of 18 to 28. During which time I overdosed twice and was hospitalized twice for attempted suicide. I had my son during this time and I can't begin to tell you the emotional neglect and abandonment this child suffered. If it had not been for my mother and older sister taking care of him, I would have lost him to the system. I know that the voraciousness of my addiction would not have let me stop using crack long enough to try and retrieve him.

By 1991, there was no semblance of who I had been before. I didn't bathe or groom myself, I couldn't. I lived to smoke crack. I stood on the corner of 96st and Macarthur Boulevard waiting for tricks begging them to date me, sometimes for as little as pocket change. I had been reduced to living like an animal, eating out of garbage cans, using the restroom where I could. My hair was matted to my head, I had a shopping cart, I stank and my feet were swollen and blistered. My skin was ashen grey and I weighed about 110 pounds. I hadn't slept in years, I was tired.

July 15, 1991, I was sitting down on the steps of an abandoned building when I heard a voice say "You have got to stop". I looked around. I didn't see anybody. I was malnourished and sleep deprived so I thought I was hallucinating. Then the voice said, "You have got to stop now"! I knew at that moment it was God speaking to me (Hebrews 3:15). I got up off those steps and for the first time in 20 years I got a good look at myself through one of the uncovered windows (Luke 15:17).

I was a block away from my mother's house but hadn't been there in 11 years except to sleep it off. I went home, took a bath and called cocaine anonymous. They gave me the name of a program and the program had a bed just for me. Thank you, Jesus. I called my father and asked him to drive me to the treatment center. Seeing what I had become really hurt him. Knowing that his beating me had driven me to the streets, driving me to the treatment center meant driving me to the solution. It would be atonement for him. He needed that. I threw some clothes in a bag, kissed my son and went into treatment.

From that day to this day I haven't found it necessary to use any mind altering substances. My mother died 2 months after I got out of treatment and on her deathbed she took my hand and promised me that if I did everything God instructed me to do that I would never use again. She also told me that day she loved me. I had wanted to hear those words from her my whole life but I knew also that she was making her peace with God. It was a bittersweet moment. I knew that she would not be coming home from the hospital. She died 2 days later. I've been clean for nearly 23 years.

In 1993 my healing began (II Kings 20:5b). I got down on my knees in my bedroom and I told God that I wanted Him to come into my life, that I wanted to know more about Him and that I wanted Him to guide me (Psalm 27:11). Right there in my bedroom, I felt the top of my head open up and I felt what seemed like a warm liquid pouring in. I told God that I wanted to understand why He came, why He died and why He needed to come back. I asked Him where I should start. He told me to start at the beginning. I started reading the bible. It took me a year to complete it but once I was done, I had fallen in love with Jesus all over again (Psalm 40:8).

Since that time I've read and studied the bible from cover to cover 6 times, and each time it reaffirms God's love for me. Everything in my life since 1991 has **not** been great. I've since then lost both my parents, I've been homeless 3 times, I've lost jobs, I've lost friends, my children didn't turn out the way I would have liked them to and I've struggled to make ends meet for the last 22 years, but the grace of God has kept me (II Corinthians 12:9). He didn't let Satan have me.

He sent me to school not for the degrees but so that I could gain access into the places where people who have been hurt like me are residing. He's given me the opportunity to tell so many people about Him and what He's done for me (Revelation 12:11). He gave my life purpose. My purpose is to inspire.

Everywhere I go, (Sunday's immediately following service) I am on a mission to inspire somebody who may want to throw in the towel. My message is to tell them to keep going. What a blessing!

I thought that being molested had been my curse. It has really been my blessing. My experiences have helped both men and women come to terms with their own trauma and get the help they need.

Remember, no matter what it looks like on the outside, "All things are working together for the good of them that love God, to them who are the called according to His purpose" (Romans 8:28).

My Song of Praise

"Amazing Grace will always be my song of praise. For it was grace that bought my liberty."
Dottie Rambo

Scripture References

Jeremiah 30:17a – For I will restore health unto thee, and I will heal thee of thy wounds, saith the Lord;

Isaiah 11:6 c – and a little child shall lead them.

Psalm 27:10 – When my father and my mother forsake me, then the Lord will take me up.

Hebrews 3:15 – While it is said, Today if ye will hear his voice, harden not your hearts, as in the day of provocation.

Luke 15:17 – And when he/she came to himself,

II Kings 20:5b – Thus saith the Lord, the God of David thy father, I have heard thy prayer, I have seen thy tears: behold I will heal thee:

Psalm 27:11 – Teach me thy way, O Lord, and lead me in a plain path, because of mine enemies.

Psalm 40:8 – I delight to do thy will, O my God:

II Corinthians 12:9 – And he said unto me, My grace is sufficient for thee; for my strength is made perfect in weakness.

Revelation 12:11 – And they overcame him by the blood of the Lamb, and by the word of their testimony;

Romans 8:28 – And we know that all things work together for good to them that love God, to them who are the called according to *his* purpose.

Personal Reflections

Poem of Deliverance
Hell?

Is that where you've been escorting me to?
You want me locked up like you?
Wait tell me, is it true, once in, I won't have
the option to try again?
Does infinite torment really begin?

Hey, I'm talking to you. Why you quiet now?
You've been "pretending" to be my best friend...
showing me the ropes, all the options I could take
to get a special dose...
And to get a feeling that I'm really doing the most?

Now you quiet and acting like a ghost....
Where's your answer to all these questions I just posed?
What, now your lips are froze I suppose?
That's it! ... Stop the ride, I want off!
Stop filming, shut the cameras off!
Delete recordings stored. I want to re-record.

It's too late...
I'm gone push play,
Take a look at the fun you've had thus far, each day
Walking and talking with me
Getting closer to me everyday
No way, do you want to throw all this away!
Hey, and don't be asking so many questions
Just continue to walk this way

Oh now you've got something to say...
I thought you had all the answers,
But obviously not today
Yes, I want to throw this crazy sin all away
No problems been solved...
I'm just hurting more and more everyday
This fun before me is but vapors,
A little wind and it flies away

Then there again I'm left,
Searching for "higher expectations" another day,
"another way"

Whatever my eyes desired, I did not keep from them...
I've looked on all the works that my hands had done
On all the labor in which I had toiled
Indeed all was vanity and grasping for the wind
There was no profit under the sun
There, was only sin

I'm tired of listening to you!
I'm going to try something new
Lord, Lord, help me I pray!
I'm aiming for delete and then record!
I want new images stored
Lord, my life is at risk
Is it really too late, is this my life bliss?
Can I get forgiveness for all of this?

I heard you call out to me
Fear not, I am here with thee
You see glimpses of who he really is;
A pretend friend playing Russian roulette with your life
The life I, "gave you"

He helped you conjure up excuses,
Pressed on your mind till you thought you were useless
Told you time would stop if, and while you do this
Laughed while he said, "you've got control of this"
He's whispered in your ear far too long;
Boasting about how you let him near, and into your home
He's told you and showed you about him,
Now let me tell you and show you, about me

I'm a doctor that's never lost a case,
I'm a father with children I embrace
I saw you before you called
I knew about it all

I love you and never want to see you fall
I know you've struggled, had unjust troubles

But I have the power to truly set you free
Surrender your troubles to me
Choose to "believe," and be free
Follow me,
Walk out of confinement
Walk out of his den
Yes, I grant you forgiveness of your sins
No sin or evil addiction will win

Written by Ruth Jackson (copyright © 2014)

Personal Reflections

Epilogue

WOW! Glory to God! As you can see these Women Up have traveled on an amazing journey to get to the place of their healing, deliverance and restoration. Along the way they shared several commonalities.

One similarity shared was how they were introduced to Jesus at a young age by mothers but especially the "grandmother" who was instrumental in many of their lives when it came to learning about God and going to church. So mothers and grandmothers our role has not changed today. We should still be leading our young children to the Lord.

The Women Up battling addictions revealed that their deliverance began when they felt sick and tired of being bound by the substances they were using just to cope with the trauma of being abused and having low self-esteem. They cried out to God for help with a sincere heart as reiterated so eloquently by our poet. And not only did God hear but He also answered them immediately.

Another common thread and the most significant one is Romans 8:28. It begins by saying **and we know**...but as many of our Women Up would say they didn't know at the time (divorce, abuse, cancer, addiction, infidelity) *that all things are working together for the good of them that love God, to them who are the called according to His purpose*, until after God had manifested himself in a great and mighty way as a healer of the sick, a mender of the broken hearted, a deliverer from danger and the God who is able to return everything back to its original state.

That same God is present to day and ready to meet you at the point of your need. It begins with John1:12; But as many as received him, to them gave he power to become the sons (daughters) of God, even to them that believe on his name. If you believe that God exists *(Loretta)* then you are ready to come to Him. Romans 10:9 says if thou (you) shalt confess with thy mouth and believe in thine heart that God raised Jesus from the dead thou (you) shalt be saved, saved from a life of ungodly living.

Pray..."Lord Jesus, forgive me for everything I have ever done that's not been according to your holy scriptures. I believe you died. I believe you were buried and I believe that God the father raised you from the dead on the third day. Right now I open the door to my heart and I receive you into my heart as my Lord and my personal Savior. Thank you, Jesus."

If you prayed that prayer with a sincere heart you are now born again *(Meredith)*. However, just like a newborn baby you need to be nursed and fed the word of God. Ask Him to lead you to a bible teaching church so that you can grow to discover your purpose and destiny. God has a plan for your life.

Amen.

Personal Reflections

Honorable Mention to *Women UP*
Not photographed on back cover

Benita Riles-Moore

Marie Evans (deceased)

Betty Mims

Gloria

About the Author/Editor

Vanessa Moore-Bulnes was born and raised in Greensboro, North Carolina where she was a faithful member of New Hope Baptist Church. She relocated to Oakland, California in 1986. She met and married her husband Elder Richard Bulnes in 1988 while serving the Lord Jesus Christ at Acts Full Gospel COGIC (Oakland). Together they have 3 beautiful children (2 sons and a daughter). In 2005 the Bulnes family was led of the Lord to join the Glad Tidings COGIC in Hayward, California.

Vanessa graduated from Mills College in 2011 with her BA in Child Development and is the owner and director of Tender Arms Family Childcare and Preschool. She is also the founder and CEO of Tender Arms Productions (TAP). In 2013 Vanessa published her first children's book *A Piece is Missing*. She believes that God is positioning her to further the gospel of Jesus Christ by using her God-given gifts and talents as a motivational speaker, an author, screenwriter and director.

Amen.

Vnessa45@yahoo.com **OR www.vanessabulnes.com**

www.ingramcontent.com/pod-product-compliance
Lightning Source LLC
Chambersburg PA
CBHW050651160426
43194CB00010B/1897